D1317400

Web Graphics for Non-Designers

Nick Boyce

Isaac Forman

Dave Gibbons

Adrian Roselli

© 2002 glasshaus

Published by glasshaus Ltd,
Arden House,
1102 Warwick Road,
Acocks Green,
Birmingham,
B27 6BH, UK

Printed in the United States
ISBN 1-904151-15-9

Web Graphics for Non-Designers

All rights reserved. No part of this book may be reproduced, stored in a retrieval system, or transmitted in any form or by any means, without the prior written permission of the publisher, except in the case of brief quotations embodied in critical articles or reviews.

The authors and publisher have made every effort in the preparation of this book to ensure the accuracy of the information. However, the information contained in this book is sold without warranty, either express or implied. Neither the authors, glasshaus nor its dealers or distributors will be held liable for any damages caused or alleged to be caused either directly or indirectly by this book.

glasshaus

labor-saving devices for web professionals

© 2002 glasshaus

Trademark Acknowledgments

glasshaus has endeavored to provide trademark information about all the companies and products mentioned in this book by the appropriate use of capitals. However, glasshaus cannot guarantee the accuracy of this information.

Credits

Authors
Nick Boyce
Isaac Forman
Dave Gibbons
Adrian Roselli

Technical Reviewers
Jon James
Dennis Kessler
Sion Lee
Drew McLellan
Adrian Roselli
David Schultz
Dawn Searcy
Don Synstelien

Indexer
Bill Johncocks

Proof Reader
Agnes Wiggers

Commissioning Editor
Chris Mills

Technical Editors
Matt Machell
Mark Waterhouse

Publisher
Viv Emery

Project Manager
Sophie Edwards

Production Coordinators
Rachel Taylor
Pip Wonson

Cover
Dawn Chellingworth

Brand Visionary
Bruce Lawson

Cover Image

The authors created the cover image for this book. Each took a different approach to digitally altering an image, then we put the results together: the ideal opportunity to show off their skills! The original photo was kindly provided by Paris Roselli; for more of his work see *http://roselli.org/paris*.

About the Authors

Nick Boyce

Nick is an art school dropout who became interested in interactive design through his involvement with photography and digital media. He has been using Photoshop since version 2, and spent a lot of time using Macromedia Director before getting involved in web design.

After working at an educational production unit developing CD-ROMs and videos, Nick went on to become a lecturer in Interactive Multimedia, and started maintaining a mailing list to keep his students informed of the most interesting design on the Web.

In 1999 he decided to build a site that assembled the information from the mailing list into a database. The result was Anarchitect.net, which has become a popular destination for designers and still maintains a mailing list. Anarchitect also functions as a space for collaborative artwork, with several projects running per year both online and offline.

Nick has been a Director at Triplezero, a web design consultancy based in Adelaide, South Australia since 1998. His goal is to buy a helicopter by the age of 25. At the time of publishing he is 24.

Isaac Forman

Isaac Forman is a Director of Triplezero in Adelaide, South Australia.

Discovering what to do, and how not to do it, has come from a variety of opportunities including a brief stunt in educational multimedia. Since the founding of Triplezero in 1998, he has provided professional Internet design and strategy service to local and international clients.

In addition, Isaac is a founder of, and prolific contributor to, the international web developer community - evolt.org.

A certified "fum-master", he whiles away much of his spare time fighting with his cat, and playing with his kitten. Distractions include digital photography, sport, and a giant tennis ball - possibly the greatest purchase in his retail history.

Isaac lives to eat, travel, and destroy opponents at Racing Scrabble.

He has eaten a spider.

Dave Gibbons

Dave Gibbons is a writer and web designer from Beaverton, Oregon, US. He recently worked for five years as a writer, Web/Intranet Designer and programmer, and usability tester at Intel.

When not losing sleep over proper web design, Dave writes humor ("humour" in the rest of the English-speaking world), novels, and screenplays.

Adrian Roselli

Adrian Roselli is a founder and partner at Algonquin Studios, located in Buffalo, New York, and also holds the moderately confusing title Vice President of Interactive Media.

Adrian has almost 10 years of experience in graphic design, web design, and multimedia development, as well as extensive experience in interface design and usability. He has been developing for the World Wide Web since its inception, when he should have been falling asleep in a video-editing suite. Adrian is also a board member of the American Advertising Federation affiliate in Buffalo (Brainstorm). One of the founders of evolt.org, Adrian has even found time to send scathing site critiques to some of the regulars on the evolt.org mailing list, which is where he spends much of his free time.

Photo by Rhea Anna

Adrian is known as "aardvark" in the wild jungles of the Internet, although if you ask him how he got that nickname, he'll just change the subject and try to steal your sandwich.

Acknowledgments:
I need to thank my family and friends for being genuinely concerned that I had been kidnapped for the duration of this writing. I thank the kind folks over at evolt.org who let me babble from a soapbox on a nearly daily basis. I thank my partners and staff at Algonquin Studios for putting up with me instead of locking me in my office. And I thank Stimulance for feeding me caffeine before I'd doze off in front of my laptop.

Table of Contents

Introduction

Not everyone who builds on the Web is a designer, either by ability or training. It's easy to forget that when someone builds an application for the Web, they have to do more than make sure the database is up, the servers are serving, and the application isn't leaking memory onto the floor. Somebody has to make the thing not just usable, but *look* good as well - not just pretty, but effectively laid out, consistent, and easy to use.

Sure, we can slap the company logo on it, put a couple of giant color bars over here, and maybe a background image of my cat (because the CEO really likes cats), and, while we're at it, find a way to make something blink. Heck, we can even just leave it as a screen of form fields nicely laid out in a column with perfect alignment and flow, a model of usability, devoid of troubling logos, and all neutral gray.

Neither of those, however, is terribly appealing to the user.

As the Web has grown, our users have come to expect more and more from sites. Five years ago a tiling background image of a bad scan of the logo from the company letterhead would have been enough to satisfy your boss, the client, and even the users. But now users are accustomed to being massaged. They go to sites with carefully chosen colors designed to reach a certain gender and age demographic, and they read text on sites where the typeface in the graphics is chosen to evoke a feeling of calm or authority.

And so new web developers can find themselves at a bit of a disadvantage.

Now, maybe you've never tried to make a pretty picture in your life, or maybe you've tried as hard as you can but you still make the sensitive souls cry when they see your sites. Believe it or not, there are rules and tricks to getting good design from terrible source imagery, colors, type, and even people. We're going to expose you to as many as we can before you pass out, dreaming of dancing through fields of chartreuse pansies under a sky of burnt umber.

And you'll never see those two colors mentioned in this book. Not twice.

Who's This Book for?

Professional web developers are a talented lot, but we can't all be expected to code perfect web applications, maintain the hardware, and design like Michelangelo (assuming he had done web design). If you find yourself in need of some training, insight, or perspective on the designs you find yourself building or maintaining, this book should be right up your alley. Using it in conjunction with some of the other glasshaus books on menu design, accessibility, CSS, etc., will almost guarantee your success and meteoric rise to web design stardom.

What Do I Need to Know?

We're assuming that you know how to code HTML, and have heard of CSS. We're also assuming that you've heard of Adobe Photoshop (maybe even used it), or other similar tools. Oh, and you'll need a browser on hand to surf really cool sites, because there are many examples of those throughout, and the printed page doesn't do justice to the clarity your monitor can produce. Although, if the printed page is clearer than your monitor, you may wish to buy a new monitor. Or at least wipe down the screen.

What's Inside?

Let's have a quick look at how the book is laid out, and see what vital knowledge is to be gleaned from each chapter.

Chapter 1: What Makes Web Graphics Work

Here we'll help you consider the benefits of simplicity in your design, flexibility in its use, consistency in its recurrence, and usability when you finally get it right.

Chapter 2: Color

Not just a primer on color theory, but enough tips and tricks so that a color-blind monkey could make nice combinations. Real-world scenarios are covered, too, like bad color choices by previous designers, and examples of good color choices from around the Web.

Chapter 3: How to Use Text Effectively

A little history, some explanation, handy rules to follow, and even some Cascading Style Sheet use. After all, your site will certainly have text in it; you may as well make it look nice.

Chapter 4: Visual Elements

This chapter touches on techniques that draw the attention of your users, as well as various forms of design elements (both function and decorative). You might not notice some of these elements on your favorite sites, but you'll definitely miss them if they're not there, and wish they weren't there when they're not right.

Chapter 5: Effective Page Layout

Even with the best colors, the best text, and the best attention grabbers, if you don't get them in the right places the site won't look as good as it should. This chapter focuses on more than just making it pretty; it's about making the whole page work together, which is critical to most web sites.

Chapter 6: File Formats and File Sizes

Now that you're ready to output those images, are you sure you've got the right format? And just how big should it be? And why do they look chunky when printed? And what should you do if you're scanning images?

Chapter 7: Tips for Using Graphics Applications

Of course, you can't really brag about your design, or roll it out, if you can't get it out of your design tools. Optimization techniques are covered here, along with cutting your images into smaller pieces (trust us, it can help).

Chapter 8: Vector Graphics for the Web

There is more to the Web than just grainy old photos. It's important to know that there is the option to create imagery that scales with your layout, and this chapter introduces that option in the form of vector graphics. The most widespread and popular format is Macromedia Flash, so we wet our toes with that before dabbling in the waters of SVG and SMIL.

Support and Feedback

Although we aim for perfection, the sad fact of book publication is that a few errors will slip through. We would like to apologize for any errors that have reached this book despite our best efforts. If you spot an error, please let us know about it using the e-mail address *support@glasshaus.com*. If it's something that will help other readers, then we'll put it up on the errata page at *http://www.glasshaus.com*.

This e-mail address can also be used to access our support network. If you have trouble running any of the code in this book, or have a related question that you feel that the book didn't answer, please mail your problem to the above address quoting the title of the book, the last 4 digits of its ISBN, and the relevant chapter and page number.

Web Support

You'll want to go and visit our web site, at *http://www.glasshaus.com*. It features a freely downloadable compressed version of the code for this book, in both `.zip` and `.sit` formats. You can also find details of all our other published books, author interviews, and more.

Introducton

1

- Basic web graphics technology and terminology
- Key concepts
- Elements of good web graphics

Author: Dave Gibbons

What Makes Web Graphics Work

You're not a designer, but you need to do some design. Maybe you're being asked to design an interface for a web app, or perhaps a web page for your department or your company. The key question for us, indeed for this entire book, is how do you make it attractive rather than looking like it was hacked together by an engineer? Do you have to discover some inner artistic genius you never knew existed, or can you make good-looking Web graphics without buying a beret?

Thankfully, there is hope for those of us who aren't Van Goghs. We can use simple artistic principles and some pretty slick applications to produce web graphics that look good and, just as importantly, function well.

Implicitly and explicitly throughout this book, we will highlight four key concepts that are important to web pages, individual graphics, and just about any graphical interface:

- Simplicity
- Usability
- Flexibility
- Consistency

This chapter acquaints you (or reacquaints you) with some of the very basic technology and terminology you'll run into in working with web graphics, followed by examples of these principles at work on real-world web sites.

Basic Web Graphics Technology and Terminology

At the most basic level, of course, using graphics on the Web requires a graphical browser, which in this context means more than "IE or Netscape and sometimes Opera". Today, you'll find graphical browsers on everything from cell phones to toasters. The idea of a "web toaster" used to be a joke, but a student recently designed a web-connected toaster that burns a graphic of the day's weather forecast onto your morning slice. It's certainly graphical, but is it a browser? Take a look at *http://news.bbc.co.uk/1/hi/sci/tech/1264205.stm* for more information on the web toaster.

The browser's job for our purposes is to present the content we give it, including graphics, text, links, and multimedia, to the user in a format that works for the user's device.

When you design a web page, you have some degree of control over how browsers lay out your content on the screen. "Some degree of control?" you might ask, incredulously. Yes, sadly, you don't have absolute control over how browsers present your content, except in the ideal environments that exist only in our utopian dreams. Until that magical future, you will have to pay some attention to cross-browser compatibility issues. This means it is sometimes necessary to use HTML coding hacks so the page works in all the browsers you're targeting.

The arrangement of content in the browser is generally referred to as layout. You can arrange content using HTML tags, multimedia programs, Cascading Style Sheets (CSS), and, if you're using XML, with XSL/XSLT. For this discussion, we'll focus on HTML layout with a bit of information about related technologies, though we'll show you examples of other techniques and technologies later in the book.

Images and Tables

There are two very common ways to use plain HTML to lay out graphics on web pages: with image tags and with tables. Image tags (also written "img tags" in this book) usually look like this:

```
<img src="http://www.glasshaus.com/header.jpg" height="76" width="615"
    alt="glasshaus logo" border="0" align="left">
```

We'll dissect this tag in somewhat excruciating detail, even though most of our readers have probably used it many times. With any luck, there are a few surprises revealed below:

```
<img
```

The first part, obviously, is the name of the tag: img, which stands for "image." Some browsers will accept image as the first word in this tag because a few older HTML specifications allowed it, but today img is the standard. We only mention it because you may see old-style `<image>` tags in the sourcecode of pages you find online.

```
src="path/filename"
```

This is the path and filename of the image, which is almost always a GIF (CompuServe's Graphical Interchange Format) or JPG (also called JPEG; both terms referring to the Joint Photographic Experts Group, which developed the standard). PNG (Portable Network Graphics, - see *Chapter 7* for more information), a very useful new format, is starting to show up on some pages, but it's rare because the bulk of older browsers don't support it and even the newer 6.x desktop browsers only support some of its features. The image could technically be just about any graphics format (a Windows bitmap, for example, or a TIFF), but in practice it will almost exclusively be GIF, JPG, and, increasingly, PNG.

```
height="pixels"
width="pixels"
```

This, fairly obviously, is the height and width of the image in **pixels** (literally "picture elements,") this is the number of dots on the screen that are taken up by the picture. (Note: this attribute can also be expressed in percentage of browser width.) What's potentially counterintuitive about these attributes is that their values aren't necessarily equal to the height and width of the original image, but are rather the height and width of the space the browser will allow for the image.

For example, you might find a picture that is 100 pixels high and 100 pixels wide, but you might want to squeeze it into a 50 by 50 pixel space on your page. You can do that without altering the source image by putting `height="50" width="50"` in the `<img>` tag. The browser looks at the height and width attributes as what you want, totally disregarding the original size of the graphic. Indeed, you could use height and width to squeeze and stretch images in any number of ways -- generally a very bad idea, but occasionally useful.

As you might guess, this can introduce a number of problems, one of which is that complex images (especially photos) resized by the browser tend to look awful. On the positive side, you can use this functionality to show small thumbnails of larger images, since the quality of thumbnails is expected to be less than that of full-size originals. This approach has a serious drawback though, since even though you'd be displaying the image in a small space, the entire image would be transferred to the browser - using as much bandwidth as if you had displayed it in all its full-sized glory. As a general rule, your height and width tags should equal the actual height and width of the source file.

```
alt="description"
```

The `alt` attribute is a text description of the image, which generally doesn't appear in the browser window at all. It is particularly useful for text-only browsers and specialized browsers for web users who are visually impaired, though it would also be seen in place of images by users who have turned graphics off in their browser (usually those with slower connections). It also appears in some graphical browsers while the graphics are downloading, and when a user hovers over a graphic. This attribute is required by most newer HTML development and checking software, which generate errors if your image tag doesn't include it. Web browsers themselves don't care whether it's present or not. This attribute is unnecessary -- even potentially counterproductive - in some specialized graphics, like purely decorative graphics or ones used only for spacing, borders, or backgrounds, so for those elements you should use attributes like this: `alt=""`

```
border="pixels"
```

If your graphic is "hot", meaning it is incorporated into a hyperlink, the border attribute tells the browser how wide to make the line around it. In most good designs, the designer sets this pixel value to zero (0), meaning the browser will not show a border around hyperlinked images.

Warning: This example includes a deprecated (but very useful) attribute -- `align`. (This functionality is now handled with the CSS "float" property. See Chapter 4.) "Deprecated" in this context means the current HTML specification (and all others since 4.0) no longer requires browsers to deal with `align` attributes, though all current browsers work with it and will continue to do so for the foreseeable future. Since there is no way to know if or when this compatibility will disappear from browsers, CSS is a better way to access this functionality.

```
align="left|right"
```

The `align` attribute tells the browser where to place a graphic in relation to a line or paragraph of text. The `<img>` tag in this case is placed within the paragraph (`<p>`) tags along with the related text. This can be useful for simple layouts, particularly where you need text to wrap around a graphic, like in a catalog or article. Though we only concern ourselves with `left` and `right` values, this attribute can accept several other values like top and bottom. The example shows how one might use the `align` attribute:

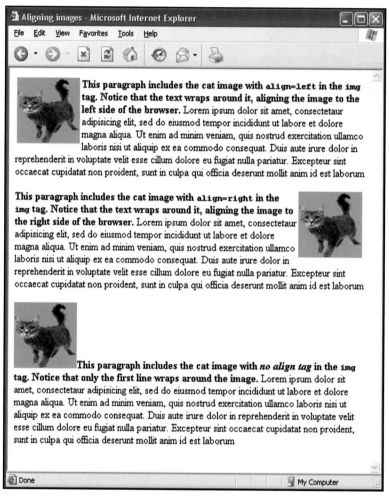

The code for this example (with the filler text omitted) looks like this:

```
<p><image src="cat.jpg" height="100" width="100" alt="Cat" border="0"
align="left"><b>This paragraph includes the cat image with <tt>align="left"</tt> in
the <tt>img</tt> tag. Notice that the text wraps around it, aligning the image to
the left side of the browser.</b></p>
```

```
<p><image src="cat.jpg" height="100" width="100" alt="Cat" border="0"
align="right"><b>This paragraph includes the cat image with <tt>align="right"</tt>
in the <tt>img</tt> tag. Notice that the text wraps around it, aligning the image
to the right side of the browser.</b></p>

<p><image src="cat.jpg" height="100" width="100" alt="Cat" border="0"><b>This
paragraph includes the cat image with <i>no align tag</i> in the <tt>img</tt> tag.
Notice that only the first line wraps around the image.</b></p>
```

Note that the only difference between the three paragraphs is the align attribute. The `<img>` tag is in the same place in each paragraph, but the appearance of the three paragraphs in relation to their attached images is radically different.

Designing with Tables

Designing with tables is probably the most common way to do complicated layouts, though it is such a maintenance and cross-browser compatibility nightmare, that it is frowned upon in the technical community, where CSS and related technologies are, for a host of reasons, preferred. The design community, concerned primarily with making pages look good today, uses tables a lot. In programming terms, designing with tables is like hacking; it's much less disciplined, robust, and forward thinking than "proper form" (CSS in this case), but it's practically unavoidable when you don't have enough time for proper form. Another, slightly less cynical, parallel between designing with tables and hacking is the fact that sometimes you have to do it to get around technological limitations. As of writing, for example, in many cases you'd need a different stylesheet for Netscape and Internet Explorer to see the same layout.

In this context, tables are invisible grids that help the web browser figure out where to place content on a screen. Like tables you'd use in Word or Excel, HTML tables have cells arranged in rows and columns. Here's a diagram of a fairly common table layout with four cells (two columns with two rows - the sketch shows lines that would normally be invisible):

1. LOGO	2. TOP NAVIGATION
3. MENU	4. CONTENT

For example:

glasshaus labor-saving devices for web professionals	Home | Products | News | Contacts | Search

Books
  Accessibility
  CMS ...
	Top news story...
	New books...

The glasshaus home page, as of this writing, uses a three-cell design, with the two top cells merged. This is called **spanning** because the attribute that tells a cell to stretch across more than one column is `colspan="number"`; the attribute of `<tr>` that tells a cell to stretch vertically to match up with more than one row is `rowspan="number"`.

On the Web, you frequently find **nested tables**, meaning that one large cell in a table (usually the CONTENT cell, number 4 in the above example) could have an entire other table inside it.

Chapter 5 goes into quite a bit more detail on designing layouts, both with tables and CSS.

Elements of Good Web Graphics

As we said at the beginning of the chapter, you'll see certain themes repeated throughout this book. Good web graphics and the page layouts into which they fit usually share most or all of these characteristics:

- Simplicity
- Usability
- Flexibility
- Consistency

This section shows some examples of real-world web sites that embody these characteristics - and some that …well, don't.

Simplicity

Once you learn to make good graphics, it's easy to get carried away, stuffing ridiculous quantities of graphical elements like animations, bullets, and buttons into a layout. But the best designs are often the simplest. The Mona Lisa doesn't need a dancing Australian menagerie in the background to be visually interesting.

Simplicity in graphic design means using only the elements necessary to convey the impression you desire. This should not be confused with "stripped down" or "utilitarian". Conveying a particular impression quite often requires visual accents, special fonts and colors, and other quite non-utilitarian touches. For example, if you want to convey "exclusiveness", you might choose a simple engraved look for your graphics, draw from a color palette that avoids harsh contrasts (*see Chapter 2*), and probably add elegant though non-functional accents on a page. Such decisions are hardly frivolous, and they don't compromise the simplicity of your design.

Take a look at the *greenhome.com* home page below . This is a relatively simple design, given the amount of information conveyed on the page. Some of the interesting touches in this design include the color scheme, which is mostly green and green-friendly colors like blue and lighter greens, and the tops of the cell borders that subtly convey the idea of "home" by imitating the shape of a roof:

This site demonstrates consistency as well, using photographs for almost all of its product graphics as well as the background in its logo. Such touches tell the user that you, as a designer, have thought about an attractive and interesting way to present the information.

This simple design from the American Museum of Natural History (*www.ology.amnh.org*) also includes a lot of information, but it is for an entirely different audience:

Notice that the large icons are all whimsical, clearly labeled, and that, even when they include photos, there is a consistency to the color palette. Considerate touches that make the site look more polished include the drop shadows "under" the icons and the use of clean, non-intrusive text for necessary links (copyright, credits, and privacy) that aren't part of the site's more fun focus. *Chapter 4* will help you with creating and using visual elements like these.

Usability

An important issue for this book is usability, but the term is rarely applied to graphics. Usability is usually linked to devices, whether those devices are physical objects or interface devices on a screen. An onscreen calculator, for example, is a device, as is a menu on a web page (see "Usable Web Menus", *glasshaus, ISBN: 1904151027*). But your choices for graphics used in your designs are informed by the same concerns as the choices you'd make in designing a telephone or a printer.

Here are some guidelines for usable web graphics:

1. If they include text, it must be clearly legible (this includes visual contrast and text and icon size).

2. If interactive, they must be easily operated and behave as your target user would expect.

3. Where it's important that graphics are distinct, like icons or other navigation elements, there should be enough space around them ("whitespace") to enable them to be easily distinguished.

4. They should load quickly.

5. They must be localizable and accessible to the disabled (including `alt` attributes).

6. They must work on multiple browsers.

Take a look at one of the models for usability online: *Amazon.com*. Even with a lot of graphics (the tabs and buttons are graphics in addition to the product pictures), it loads quickly and manages to stay uncluttered. Some of the simple graphical touches you might notice on this page include: the tops of the tabs and left-side navigation boxes use rounded corners to match the rounded buttons; the colors are very complementary and usually include enough contrast between text and background to maintain good readability. Notice that in the tabs, where the text is small, the letters get muddier and therefore more difficult to read, particularly the soft yellow "WELCOME" on the dark blue background:

Another usability principle at work here to varying degrees is the idea of making your mouse targets very distinct from one another and large enough to hit easily. The menu on the left side includes a generous amount of space between the options, making its options easy to hit. The *Go* button on the *Search* function, however, is small. Only the fact that there is plenty of empty space on each side of it keeps it easily accessible.

There's a visual trick on this page that relates to mouse targeting: the rounded corners on the tabs. If a user wanted to click the "Software" tab, for example, they'd be more likely to click near the middle of it rather than the edges, simply because the middle looks thicker. Usability tests show this kind of consideration prevents users from clicking near the borders, where they would be more likely to make a mistake and select the wrong option. The logic goes like this: if the tabs were square, there would be no real focal point for a user to shoot at. The user might move the mouse across the screen just far enough to cross from one tab to the next and then click the button. By rounding the top corners, you create a visual sense that you need to keep moving the mouse until you get closer to the middle. Technically, you could still click the first pixel inside the tab, but psychologically you'll want to click more toward the "thicker" part of the tab, away from the edge. Go to Amazon and mouse across those options to see how you naturally react to these visual cues.

NASA's Earth Observatory site, found at *earthobservatory.nasa.gov*, uses plenty of space (so to speak!) around its icons for usability's sake, and for an attractive layout. The meanings of most graphics are clear, and the style is consistent, using photo-realistic images with drop shadows for the permanent buttons. Overall, the site is able to convey a very polished look with a simple graphical approach:

The page uses captions very well, explaining some of the more mysterious graphics (what is that "missions" graphic?) rather than making the user guess their meanings. Labels are very important in this type of graphic. This is something you'll learn in designing graphics: a picture, particularly an icon, has no *universal*, *intuitive* meaning. It may be something most people understand, even something that 95% of people understand, but it doesn't take long to find someone who will tell you your perfect icon for "trash can" looks like a speedboat.

The ZC Sterling site is something of a classic among un-usable web sites - it's an all-time favorite on "Web Pages that Suck" *(webpagesthatsuck.com)*. The graphics are lovely and engaging, but they don't mean anything, unless you're patient enough to click on each one. The trouble, of course, is that nobody is that patient. Users will visit other insurance/mortgage companies (can you tell from the graphical style that this is a finance company?) rather than wander around in this beautiful mess:

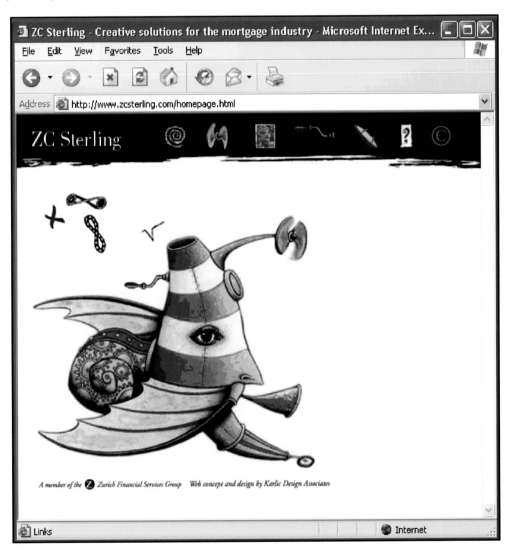

Flexibility

If everyone in the world used a computer like yours, a browser like yours, and a screen like yours (not to mention speaking a language like yours), flexibility wouldn't be an issue. Of course, they don't. Increasingly, you can't even count on them using a PC or a PC-like device. So your design has to take into account the idea that some people won't be able to read text embedded in your graphics. The easiest way out is to provide a text-only option for your site, but a more elegant solution is creating device-specific alternative pages or stylesheets that lay out your pages for delivery in other formats.

In short, an increasingly important factor in graphic design is how well your site works *without* graphics.

The king of flexibility online is *Google.com*. Look at how simply the site changes for use on a simple WAP phone. Contrast this with Amazon's presentation on the same emulator. Can you even recognize Amazon here? Notice that this emulator helpfully warns us at the bottom that the Amazon page is not optimized for use on a mobile phone:

Always test your public sites with a mobile phone or emulator if your target audience is even slightly likely to access it from their mobile. It's also a good idea to test pages with a text-only browser like Lynx, which can show you if you've inadvertently left off an important `alt` attribute or otherwise made your design inaccessible to people who use alternative browsers. (There is no web toaster emulator, as far as we know.)

Consistency

One of the easiest and best ways to make your graphics usable and convey the desired impression is to keep them consistent throughout a page, or an entire site. This means deciding on a consistent color palette, font set, and a consistent "feel" to the graphics. For example, if you use photo-realistic images for most of your graphics, other graphics should also look photo-realistic and design elements like borders should look elegant and unobtrusive. If your site is more easy-going, you might have a "cartoon feel," so not only would full-size graphics be cartoons, but other elements like borders could look like crayon or wobbly pencil lines. It's easy to violate this principle, particularly when a site uses banner ads or other graphics from external sources.

In the example below *(dlp.tc.Columbia.edu)*, the page is relatively consistent with its use of a mildly slanted parallelogram in several places, a consistent feel to the fonts, and its colors:

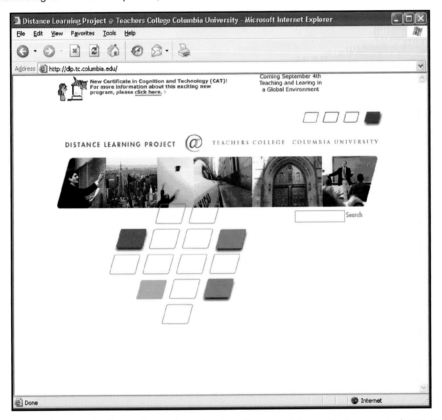

The photographic focal point fits well, particularly since its overall frame is the same shape as other elements on the page. But if you look in the upper left corner, you'll see a piece of cartoon clipart, ruining the effect of the entire page. It would be much better if this element were cordoned off with a visible border so that it didn't look so out of place. Users expect banners to have a different visual style than other elements of a page (even though this example isn't a banner as such), so that kind of simple modification would restore a great degree of consistency to the whole page.

Queen Mary's official site *(www.queenmary.com)* consistently uses a 1920s-era font for its bold elements. It is also consistent in its use of photos and photo-realistic art. Overall, these simple touches, applied consistently, make an attractive site:

The Blue Raven site, found at *www.blueravenco.com*, has a very attractive design, which should be no surprise considering it is a site for an art dealer. The fonts are consistent, as are the colors. That is, until you get see the glaring yellow "M Leave a message" button sticking out, as they say, like a sore thumb. The font is inconsistent with the rest of the page, the shape is inconsistent with other shapes on the page, and there's not even a reasonable excuse for drawing attention to it, such as that element being either extremely important or an industry standard icon (it also differs from the "Send Us Feedback" button on the same page). Here we see again how one element can cause problems for an otherwise very attractive site:

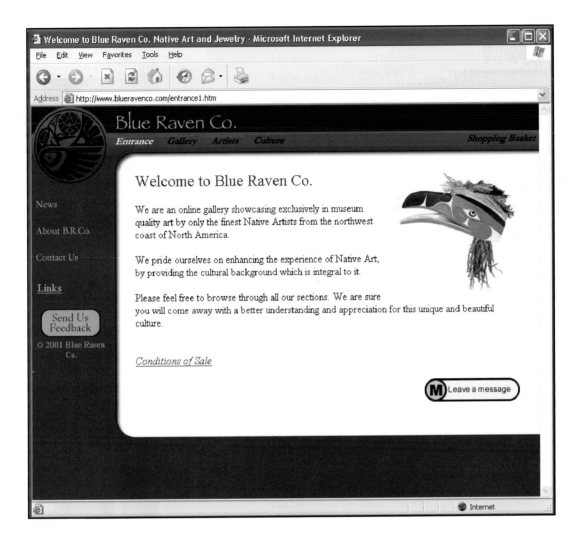

Summary

There's a lot to think about when you set out to make attractive and usable Web graphics, but that's the point - *to think about what you're designing.* Your thoughtfulness will be seen by user as considered design, just as a slapdash approach will inevitably show up as careless design.

You may have to reconsider basic assumptions you've made about technologies you've been using for years. If you follow good design guidelines, emphasizing simplicity, usability, flexibility, and consistency, you'll catch the mistakes that so often ruin otherwise good designs.

2

- Color theory
- Choosing a color scheme
- Good color practice
- Incorporating color

Author: Isaac Forman

Using Color

Color performs a significant function in our world, providing an effective means of communicating a message. The skin markings on animals, and interpretations of these, influence thinking and alter actions. In everyday life, the color of lights, signs and other signals give us compelling directions. On the Web, circumstances are much the same.

"color is a sensation and not a substance."

History of Color Photography (1947) Joseph Friedman

In the hands of a web designer, color is a powerful tool. With grounding in fundamental color theory, it is a competitive advantage and an asset to clients. Strong reactions to color from the audience of a site can assist in such things as brand confidence, sales growth and readership. Attaining or improving on these crucial goals can bring promotions, awards and referrals of new clients.

A well-considered color scheme is frequently the difference between a reasonable web site, and a great web site. It can also mean the difference between a great site and an unusable site, if the scheme used is too outrageous.

To ignore the benefits of intelligent use of color is to limit you as a professional, and to also limit the sites that you produce.

Color branding is a distinct afterthought for a great number of sites on the Web today. While for the vast majority of sites there is not always the budget, time allowance or skill available to devote an army to brand management, ensuring that your color choices are inline with the style and goals of your branding is a quick and straightforward step forward that should not be ignored.

For those with a background in artistic pursuits, harmonious color selection comes instinctively, while for others it can be an unnatural process. The following guide to basic color theory and color schemes will give the uninitiated a chance to catch up. Also in this chapter, you will learn about how to choose an appropriate color scheme, how to use color on the Web (and the various traps to watch for), as well as the importance of color consistency.

With this knowledge, creating attractive sites and drawing inspiration from everyday life is achievable.

Color Theory

At the heart of basic color theory lie the three Primary colors: red, yellow, and blue:

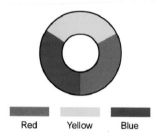

Combining these gives the Secondary colors of green, orange, and purple:

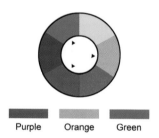

Subsequently, going a level deeper and the combination of a Primary and Secondary color gives us the Tertiary colors of red-orange, red-purple, blue-purple, blue-green, yellow-green, and yellow-orange:

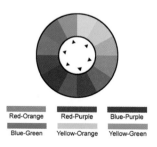

Tertiary colors are a form of intermediate colors, which are the result of further combinations from the color wheels presented. A color wheel shows these hues (as you will learn soon, a hue is a pure color) from which every other color is created.

Every other color available for use on the web is a variation in tone, tint, or shade, each of which you will learn more about shortly. Combining natural hues with the neutral colors black and white (and the grays in between), gives these variations. From the definition of a hue that follows, you will learn that these neutrals have no hue.

Color Terms to Know

Hue: A hue is a pure color with no black or white added. It is the feature of a color that allows it to be identified as, say, red or blue:

Intensity: Also known as saturation or chromaticity, intensity describes the identifiable hue component of a color. A blue with RGB (0,0,255) is considered intense (or completely saturated, and high in chromaticity) and 100% saturated. A gray, however, has no identifiable hue, and is termed achromatic with 0% saturation:

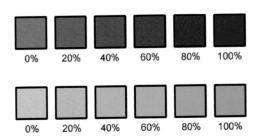

| 0% | 20% | 40% | 60% | 80% | 100% |

| 0% | 20% | 40% | 60% | 80% | 100% |

Shade: A shade is a hue with black added:

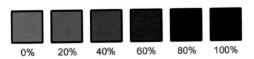

| 0% | 20% | 40% | 60% | 80% | 100% |

Tint: A tint is a hue with white added:

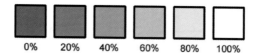

Tone: A tone is a hue with gray added (tending towards neutrality), or a hue with some strength of its complementary color added:

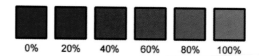

The results of adding a hue to its complement generally appear richer than the addition of straight neutrals:

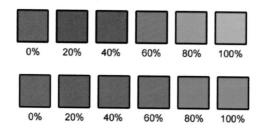

RGB and CMYK: RGB and CMYK are color spaces relied upon by designers every day. The RGB space, representing red, green, and blue, will be the most familiar to web developers. Understanding the two, though, is as easy as comprehending the differences. RGB is additive color used by electronic displays (and curiously, the human eye) where red, green, and blue light creates the colors we see on screen. The default black you see on screen is simply a deficiency of all of these colors. Conversely, combining the three gives white.

CMYK, on the other hand, is subtractive and standard in the printing industry. A blank page, for example, is white and reflects all colors. Adding cyan, magenta, and yellow to the page actually subtracts from the light reflected. Combining cyan, magenta, and yellow does not give black, and so black is added independently. It is represented as the letter K to avoid confusion with blue.

Due to limitations of printing with ink, the CMYK color space is actually smaller than that of RGB. Photoshop, for example, has the ability to warn you of colors in the RGB space that will not survive a conversion to CMYK As such, when converting from RGB to CMYK, some colors are lost (you may have seen Photoshop's "out of gamut" warning which is telling you that this is occurring). Nonetheless, for the most part web developers will not need to step outside of RGB, other than to occasionally convert corporate color values, and should not be troubled by this.

Alpha: The term "alpha" refers to a further value within a color definition, and determines transparency. As you may be well aware, a GIF provides support for transparency, but the value at a given pixel must be either fully transparent or opaque. Forward-looking formats such as PNG provide better alpha bearing, but are not as supported by browsers such as the GIF and JPEG formats.

Choosing a Color Scheme

Successful online colors schemes are chosen to support the goals of a site, be they to strengthen branding, increase sales, or maintain readership. An intelligent color scheme not only looks good, but also creates a feeling amongst the audience. If you choose a scheme that does not support your goals, then you have fallen short of the potential of your site.

Color can assist in achieving goals by suggesting an environment that visitors can identify with. For example, a site selling baby products could use a vibrant scheme that parents would appreciate as being a bright and positive influence, while an art gallery could employ a black background that presented a feeling of sophistication and luxury.

While there is more to be considered than just making an attractive site, knowing how to create a harmonious color scheme is a strong start. Harmonious color schemes are derived systematically from the basic color wheel of tertiary colors. For the purposes of this grounding, they are of four types: monochromatic, analogous, complementary, and triadic. Using each, it is best to aim for a selection of three or four distinct hues, coupled with neutrals.

Monochromatic

Monochromatic color schemes are derived from a single base color, and extended using its shades and tints (that is, a color modified by the addition of black and white. Consider, for example, a saturated green (RGB {0,255,0}). The swatches each show the pure hue in the center, with white being added to the right, and black to the left. In each case, the core hue remains identical.

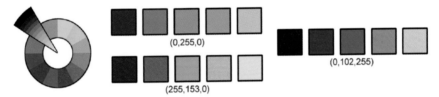

(0,255,0)

(0,102,255)

(255,153,0)

As you can see from the wheel above, by altering the value of this pure hue we can create colors that cleanly support the original.

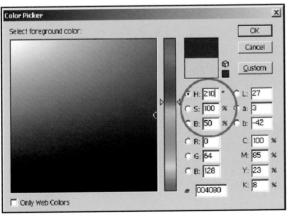

In Photoshop, changing the value next to the **H** in the color picker can alter hues. Adjusting the brightness is done using the value alongside the **B.** The **S** signifies the saturation of your color. The latter two values are measured as a percentage, while the hue is measured in degrees, positioning the hue on a color wheel.

This site bases its scheme around a feminine pink. The monochromatic scheme avoids detracting from the key, full-color photographs that sell the product.

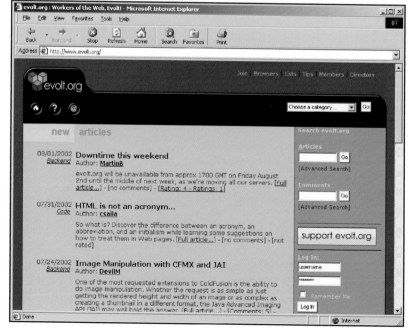

Here, the monochromatic scheme keeps the focus on the content within the site.

A monochromatic color scheme is often considered for sites where content is of extreme importance, or when the opinions presented are of a moderate nature. It can give a site a clean and classic look, but also provides excellent opportunities to let full color photographs dominate. Monochromatic schemes are often appropriate for serious political and business sites such as those of some banks, where instilling customer confidence, in their experience, is important. They are also highly suited to fashion sites where the understated monochromatic scheme supports the branding, but nevertheless allows the photographical elements to provide a focus.

Analogous

Selecting colors adjacent to one another on the color wheel creates a scheme of analogous colors. For example, orange, red-orange, and yellow-orange would be an analogous scheme with a fiery influence. The swatches below are based around an analogous set of colors with supporting tones and neutrals. Applying the first swatch, for example, could see the white being used on the darkest orange as a highlight, or used as a background color for a content region.

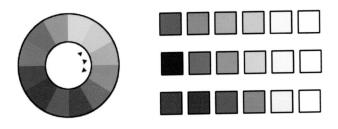

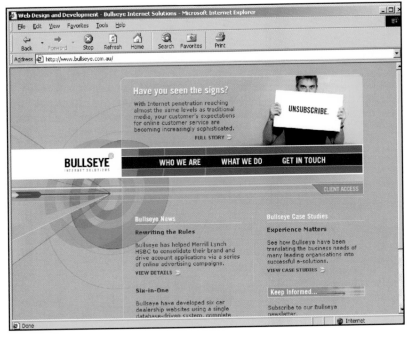

Bullseye, providers of Internet services, use a largely orange scheme that is a direct contrast to the blue used heavily by firms providing professional services to corporate clients.

Winery Hill Smith Estate has used a combination of heritage greens, accompanied by an analogous straw color that maintains the natural feel.

An analogous color scheme can provide a truly harmonious feel to a site with a balanced visual experience. Using one of the colors predominantly will establish a solid base for your site layout, while the partnering colors maintain the soothing appearance. Examples of analogous themes are readily present in nature, from the blue-greens of the ocean to the red-browns of natural timber. Such schemes are useful in presenting resource companies as solid and hardworking or environmental organizations as earthy and resourceful.

Complementary

Selecting colors opposite each other on the color wheel creates a scheme of complementary colors. The opposite of the primary blue, as per the diagram below, is orange. For purple, the complementary is yellow, and so on. In each of the swatches below, the two tones on the left complement the two on the right.

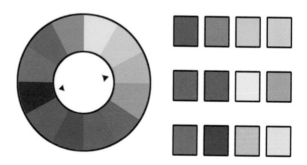

Once you have mastered selecting complementary colors, it may be time to experiment with the **double complement**, that is, choosing two sets of complementary colors. Alternatively, consider the **split complement** that chooses a hue and two colors adjacent to its alternate. The diagram below shows an example of color positioning for a double complement (left) and split complement (right) on a color wheel:

Remember that simplicity is one of the key components of successful web design. There is nothing to be ashamed about in using a scheme in which you have confidence rather than striking out into fresh color ground simply for the sake of it.

Fusion are new media developers. Their site presents a bold and confident appearance with a striking complementary combination.

Complementary color schemes can give sites a vibrant feel. Sites designed to appeal to children often use these themes to appear exciting and dynamic. Such choices also appeal to parents buying for their children, who understand that a lively environment can be a positive influence on a growing mind. A complementary scheme commonly used is the red and green combination invoked by retailers during the Christmas season. You should be conscious, though, of the way in which complementary colors can behave near each other. Color behavior is discussed at a later point in this chapter.

These combinations can also present a subdued feel if de-saturated hues are used. Also, be aware that the screen-space devoted to your main colors can substantially alter your final effect. As an example, a page that is almost entirely monochromatic, but with a slight addition of titles or features in a bright complement can create a punchy effect without looking like it is an entertainment site for children.

Triadic

The triad approach to selecting colors involves picking from the points of an equilateral triangle within a color wheel. That is, choosing three colors that are equidistant from each other. In Photoshop, choosing triadic associates for your base color is as easy as adding or subtracting 120° from the hue value. For example, a red with hue angle of 0° should be accompanied by a green of 120° and a blue of 240°.

For the advanced, an **alternative complement** is a four-hue scheme that adds a complement of one hue to a triad. Another four-hue scheme is the **tetrad** - four colors selected from the points of a square within a color wheel. Both are shown in the diagram below.

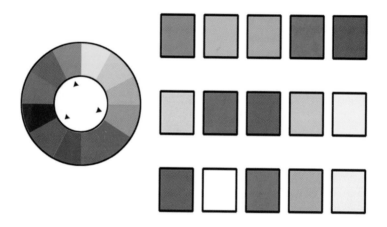

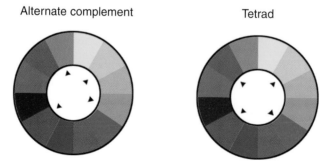

Alternate complement   Tetrad

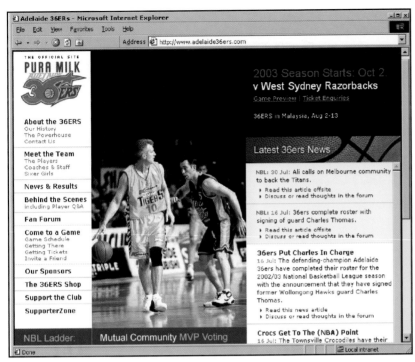

The Adelaide 36ers use the bold primary colors of blue, red, and yellow, drawing directly from corporate colors.

Sites employing the contrasting colors of triadic schemes still retain some sense of harmony, while bringing a lively feel to an online presence. If you are looking for a unique theme to create a stir for the site of an illustrator, a satirical magazine, or a quirky band, then one of these color sets is definitely worth a try. Also try de-saturating colors somewhat to maintain a unique look, but with a more restrained effect.

A Starting Place for your Scheme

A color scheme is often anchored to a seldom-altered brand. Consider a few of the more memorable color choices and schemes on the Web today, and while you'll find that some of the sites have undergone substantial redesigns, very few have deviated from the colors that their audience has come to recognize as supporting their positioning.

The Register has grown to establish its place as bold and opinionated with a red that could be no more self-confident.

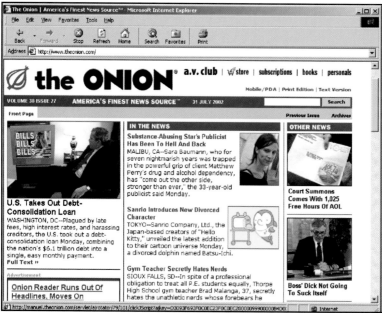

The Onion has selected a medium green - half way between the heritage green of an established news source, and the livelier green of an onion shoot, reflecting its unusual and fresh attitude to humor.

Over many years, IBM has defined the blue of the business world, a color that exudes an impression of stability and careful dealings. Yellow is used as a complementary accent.

Target is one of the most recognizable commercial users of the red and white combination. Here they have added a fresh complementary green to introduce product for a new season.

When creating a design for a client large enough to have an established brand, existing components should be considered first.

Corporate Colors

The first priority in the majority of color decisions should be consideration of current corporate colors. Opting for colors complementary or analogous to those within the corporate scheme ensures an eye-pleasing result.

tommy.com - partial triadic

bluefly.com - analogous

wishlist.com.au - monochromatic

caltex.com.au - complementary

motown.com - monochromatic

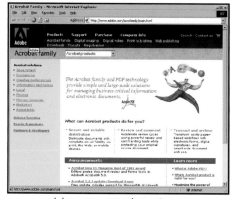

adobe.com - complementary

A broad range of colors can accompany a single corporate hue, whether analogous, complementary, monochromatic, or triadic in relation. Your exact choice should depend on the industry, positioning, and goals of the site in development. Basing a color scheme on the familiar blue of the IBM logo (pictured below) could potentially take one of the four paths shown here:

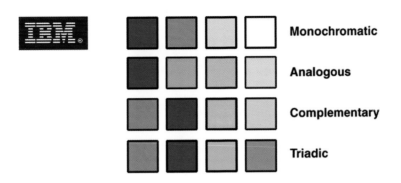

If the identity colors are analogous, it is easy to extend the scheme to a third color adjacent on the color wheel. Similarly, in the event of two colors having the same source hue, selecting a third shade or tint to form a monochromatic association is easy.

Sourcing Colors

The identity design firm contracted to create the style guide for your company or client has generally defined the corporate colors. In the case that no one has them noted somewhere convenient, you should look to contact the designers. More often than not, these colors will be provided as Pantone values.

Pantone color numbers are a proprietary system created to guarantee accurate representation of color in printed and other physical materials such as textiles. They are an essential part of life in a professional design company, but are of somewhat less use online, where differences in monitor quality, gamma correction, viewing conditions, video hardware, and user preferences combine to make the Web the occasionally impossible place we know and love. Regardless, where budget (and patience!) permits, kicking off with the correct Pantone colors is a good move.

The values provided to you may correspond to any number of standards, so you might need extra information, but the more popular of those available is generally Pantone Uncoated.

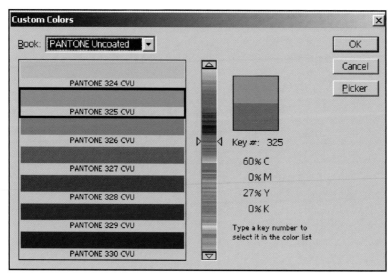

To translate your Pantone colors to your RGB working space in Photoshop, you will need to open the color picker, select the custom button at the right hand side, and then confirm that your color standard is selected in the *Book* dropdown box. Then enter the color digits and allow the dialog to auto-select your color, before choosing to return to the Picker. This will give you your RGB triplet and, in more recent versions of Photoshop, the color in hexadecimal format. This screenshot shows the *Custom Colors* dialog box.

In the case of designers having disappeared and Pantone values being unavailable, color picking from a digital file, such as an EPS (Encapsulated PostScript file), is your next option. All quality graphics applications have a tool (the eyedropper in Photoshop, for example, highlighted in the image at the right) that allows "sampling" of the color value at any given pixel.

Logo: Marks and Logotypes

Unfortunately, it is not uncommon to encounter genuine lost artwork or client apathy and be forced to work from nothing but a printed logo (such as a letterhead). If faced with this scenario, you should aim for a "best guess" by comparing your printed source with an on-screen color picker until satisfied with your selection. This, however, is an absolutely final alternative. Do not forget to consider calibrating your monitor to use a gamma correction similar to that likelt to be used by a majority of your eventual audience. Gamma correction is discussed briefly at a later stage of this chapter.

Given an undefined corporate color or set of colors, adapting a scheme from a logo is a sensible second priority and can be built upon using the methods outlined previously. When caught with a disassociated scheme within a brand, perhaps selected by misguided designers, all hope is not lost. A resourceful designer will choose and emphasize one hue. Techniques to avoid affecting your scheme with the inharmonious colors remaining in your logo are discussed later in this chapter. After selecting one hue and treating it as a base element, choosing either a complementary or analogous support cast is straightforward.

Feature Images

Drawing a color scheme from prominent hues in a featured image can be a successful back-up option in a number of cases. Two such situations are:

Weak or no brand: Of the many commercial sites on the Web, a great number do not possess a recognizable brand, or perceive little need for an investment in an image of this sort. Examples of sites falling into this category are small clients such as automotive businesses, tradespeople, artists (whether visual or audio), and freelance programmers. Rather than being a condition to be ashamed of, it is nothing less than a blank canvas and an exciting opportunity. Basing your color scheme on a catchy or otherwise key image gives you instant direction.

Strong promotion: Instances of important promotions, or in cases where the "concept" of the site far outweighs the brand recognition, are other opportunities to use a feature image as a base for your theme. Examples of sites for which this could be appropriate include travel agencies, auction sites, and interior decorators.

Selecting colors from a feature image is as simple as color picking for inspiration by choosing one of the more dominant colors, and then seeking an analogous or complementary union.

The eyedropper tool available in most graphics packages provides a choice of a point sample (single pixel), or a color average over a 3x3 or 5x5 pixel sample. These latter options prove quite useful if you are attempting selection of a green from a shrub, blue from the sky, or brown from a timber texture.

A swatch showing the regions in which the eyedropper tool was used to source insight accompanies the screenshot below. In this case, the interior design company Key Designs & Developments possessed corporate stationery using various strengths of silver and transparent plastic stock. Translating this to the web was a difficult task, and so an olive color and lighter tint were color-picked from the courtyard greenery. Then a complementary red-brown was selected from the feature candles in the other highlighted photograph.

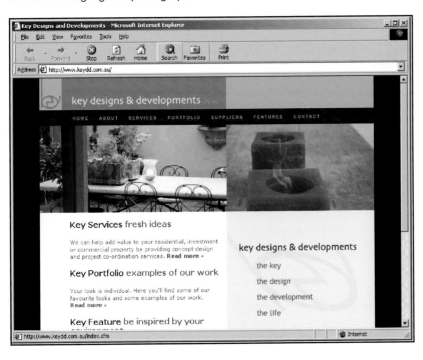

Other Sources of Inspiration

An alternative to the feature image source of color schemes is the world around you. Thousands of opportunities exist throughout nature, industrial design, lighting effects, and the fashion world that can inspire you to choose a scheme and even supporting photographical elements. With a blank canvas and a target feeling for your audience, finding motivation is painless.

Much of this is easier to learn through practice rather than pure instruction. Use your knowledge of color theory to choose and create your schemes. Consider the following photographs and the

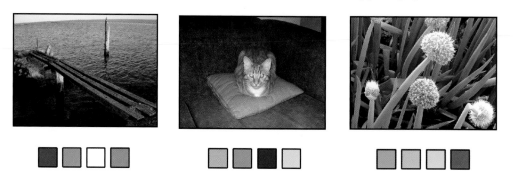

swatches they inspired.

Good Color Practice

An artist is often challenged by boundaries, and the Web presents some troubling limitations in the form of bandwidth compromises, varying screen resolutions, and video hardware.

A number of these restrictions relate directly to the realm of color online. A GIF image, for example, increases in size with image complexity and the palette used. Gamma correction defaults change from platform to platform, and contrast can vary across different display types. And to really keep everyone on their toes, the capabilities of video hardware from system to system (most often the number of colors they display) can differ by a substantial order of magnitude.

Web Safe Palette

At a time when 8-bit video cards were commonplace in computers, there arose amid web developers the murky head of the browser-safe palette. First publicized by Lynda Weinman on her web site, lynda.com, known as the web-safe palette, it outlined a set of 216 colors considered safe for usage across the PC and Mac platforms, and Internet Explorer and Netscape Navigator browser applications.

Many among the developer crowd will know that an 8-bit display is capable of showing 256 colors. Of these, the respective PC and Mac platforms reserve 40 for system usage, leaving a subset of 216 that are available on both.

The web-safe palette is not difficult to remember. Its RGB triads specified in decimal format are simply the 256 values (0 is the 256th), spaced evenly over five intervals (- that is, divisible by 51). These are: 0, 51, 102, 153, 204, and 255. HTML also supports color values in hexadecimal format, and these intervals represented in this format are 00, 33, 66, 99, CC, and FF.

Therefore, a color is web-safe if its decimal representation has each RGB value equal to any of the values divisible by 51. {51,102,255}, {0,204,204}, and {255,153,51} are web-safe colors, while {51,102,104}, {43,72,60}, and {52,103,154} are not. In hexadecimal, #CCFF00, #669900 and #00FFFF are safe, whereas #008822, #FC3293, and #4400CC are not.

The palette itself is included below for your reference. You will notice that the selection of colors is extremely limiting; it contains a small number of light and dark colors, and is particularly useless if you are considering a scheme incorporating muted and tinted colors.

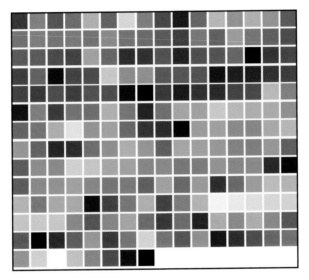

Today the concept of the web-safe palette is largely in the past, along with the now antiquated 8-bit video cards. The palette was first published in around 1996, but currently usage of 8-bit video hardware sits at around 3% of users (statistic according to *TheCounter.com*).

Color depth	Percentage
6-bit	47%
32-bit	38%
24-bit	10%
8-bit	3%
Other (unknown, 4-bit, etc)	2%

To compound the issue, however, the 16-bit hardware supporting high color, and used by around half of all users, has a color set that is not a subset of the 24-bit true color palette in the same way that the 8-bit and web-safe palettes are. Because of this, color shifts arise for this large percentage of users when 194 of the 216 supposedly web-safe colors are used. A color shift is a difference in rendering of color. While a user with 24-bit video hardware might see your colors as you intended, others with less advanced hardware (and thus a restricted palette) might see a "similar" color. This shift will be quite obvious to many users.

Unfortunately, in some browsers these shifts of an unsupported color to its nearest supported neighbor can occur differently for HTML-defined color and image-defined color. This leaves 22 colors that are really web safe. If you are interested in learning a bit more about this, Webmonkey have an article which will fill you in: *Death of the Websafe Color Palette*, see *http://hotwired.lycos.com/webmonkey/00/37/index2a.html?tw=design*

In more relevant terms, this means that attempting seamless transitions with web-safe colors between the background color of an image, and the background color of a table cell (for example), is not entirely recommended. Approximately half of your users will probably witness a visible seam.

Ultimately, the web-safe palette is not entirely web-safe, and subsequently, adherence to its color-range is now a less common practice.

Best Practice

The palette and techniques you use are dependent on your audience and the assumptions you make about them. You have a number of options:

- **Play it safe, really safe**: If your brand and site image is a low priority, and you are looking for a challenge, then working within the 22 colors of the really safe color palette might be worth considering.

- **Stick with web safe**: To keep everyone mostly happy, you can work to the web-safe palette. The larger group of 16-bit users will experience some color shifting, but the fewer 8-bit users should be saved from the far less attractive dithering. Dithering occurs when the video hardware of a computer attempts to replicate an unsupported color by using a pattern of two other colors.

- **Use transparent backgrounds**: If your GIF only has to blend seamlessly with one HTML background color, then making the equivalent color in your GIF transparent will remove many typical lines of stitching concerns.(since the background color shows through, there is no seam between the HTML color and the image color.)

- **Keep GIFs and HTML colors separate**: Since the color shifting which occurs for the majority of typical web audiences results from differences in color handling of images and HTML colors, separating the two within your page layout will prevent users from noticing seams. Nevertheless, some of the color shifting will be noticeable to the point that differences are discernable, even when colors are not adjacent. Testing will help you find out which colors are susceptible to this.

For most designs, using the restrictive 22-color palette will not be an option. With that in mind, the most sensible action would be a combination of the remaining techniques.

- Where possible, use web-safe colors for backgrounds of pages and tables.

- To minimize visible seams, make GIFs adjacent to an HTML background color partially transparent.

- When designing, keep in mind that separating GIFs with background colors from their HTML background equivalents removes the possibility of noticeable color shifting.

- Know your audience, and design to keep your site attractive for the majority.

Of course, regardless of the method you use you should always test your design on as many platforms, browsers, and color depths as are available to you. There may be valuable sacrifices you can make with your layout to remove seams and dithering.

PC vs. Mac

Gamma correction can be an issue when designing for the Web, and has a particular effect on the appearance of colors you use. Gamma correction, generally speaking, is a modification to the color saturation and brightness as displayed on your monitor, and can vary significantly from computer to computer. The most notable difference exists between Macintosh and PC computers. Macs usually adjust to a gamma correction factor of 1.8, while most PCs begin with a darker default of 2.5.

So, how does this affect your work? If you are designing on a PC for an audience featuring a majority of Mac users, you should adjust your gamma correction to emulate the default Mac of 1.8. On the contrary, if designing on a Mac for a PC-heavy audience, it would be advisable to temporarily bend your gamma correction to something closer to 2.5. Finally, given that most of the people on the Web are using PCs, your gamma for a very general audience should be set to 2.5 also.

However accurate you might believe your gamma correction to be, if you are not designing to best represent your color scheme and image brightness to the majority of your audience, you are contravening one of the web commandments : design with the audience in mind!

Previewing your design with the default gamma correction settings of another platform is a straightforward process. For example, in Photoshop for Windows *CTRL-Y* allows you to easily toggle between the default, and your current proof setting.

- You can learn more about gamma correction at: *http://cgsd.com/papers/gamma_intro.html*

- For Mac users, a simple gamma correction toggle is available from: *http://www.thankyouware.com/gammatoggle.html*

- PC users can try PowerStrip from EnTech Taiwan: *http://www.entechtaiwan.com*

LCD vs. CRT

Frequent computer users would be familiar with the differences between LCD and CRT screens used by today's computer users. The difference that first and foremost affects your decisions in creating a site is of contrast. When viewing a Liquid Crystal Display, commonly used in notebook/laptop screens, at the usual angle, near-white colors such as cream, beige or silver can appear indistinguishable from white. This is rarely a crucial issue, as vital components such as text never appear as light cream on white. It can, however, create unintended effects as cell backgrounds, alternating table row colors, and watermarks disappearing into your background color, and it is something to be aware of. With a vague audience definition, it is unlikely to trouble you, but if you are charged with designing a resource specifically intended for users of laptops, then keep an eye out and be sure to check your color choices on both CRT and LCD screens.

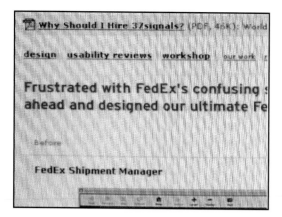

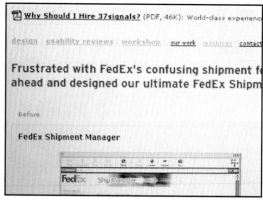

CRT: Soft butter-colored background provides focus for a key headline

LCD: The focus is lost as the cream background disappears.

Consistency

Consistency is key to good color practice on the Web, reinforcing brand recognition and familiarity. Steady usage of color makes users feel at home, and eases the ability of a visitor to recognize when they have shifted outside the realm of your site. Other sites may have different standards with regard to security, member privacy, sales policies, and quality of product. It is important that you make it as easy as possible for users to recognize their movement outside of your zone of control.

With an increase in the strength of a brand and its color association, the importance of color consistency also increases.

You will probably be familiar with the following examples of strong color association and uniformity:

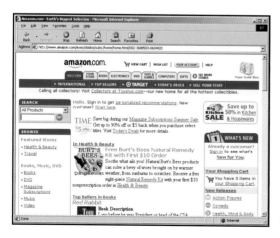

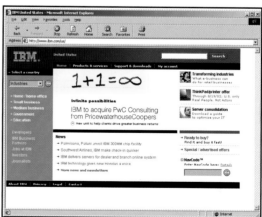

There are some methods that you can employ which will simplify the process of standardizing your colors.

Saving Palettes

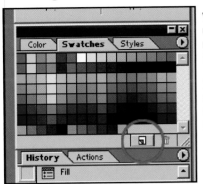

While designing your site templates, specifying key colors and using these as a source for others is as simple as clicking the new swatch icon on your color palette in Photoshop when you have the desired color as your foreground selection.

Photoshop also has the ability to save custom palettes, allowing you to maintain a single source file, and thus consistency. These preferences can be found within the layer options. Other graphics packages have similar features.

Shades and Tints

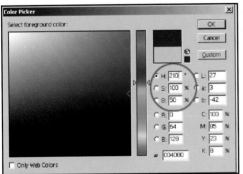

While still in your preferred layout application, selecting shades and tints from your core hues keeps you from moving even slightly out of the range of your scheme.

In the screenshot to the left, you will note that while selecting a color from those available, the hue value (H) does not change. You can still change the saturation of the color by altering the percentage of S, or the brightness (B).

Style Sheet Comments

When your site moves further into production, comments in stylesheets are an excellent way of maintaining your custom palette. Awareness among your production team is also a good idea, guaranteeing that no one will ever source a color incorrectly, for example by second-generation color picking from a lossy JPEG screenshot. Any further colors required within the site should be sourced from, and added to, this record. An example follows:

```
/*

Base color scheme for Client X:
Core blue: #xxxxxx
Table header: #xxxxxx
Table row: #xxxxxx
Table row alternate: #xxxxxx
Complementary orange link: #xxxxxx
Faded orange (visited link): #xxxxxx
Strong orange header: #xxxxxx

*/
```

This is also a useful reminder for times when you come to revisit a site you designed yourself some time ago.

Simplicity

Color simplicity is an often-overlooked facet of successful web design. Almost every web user will recall seeing a garish rainbow effect applied to text or a background. Doing something simply because you are able to is hardly justification for an action. A few might think it fancy, but the majority will recognize it for what it is - illegible grandstanding. Considered implementation will more likely be rewarded with success, whether that be a more appreciated design, or a recognized brand.

Showing restraint with your color selection is a good start. The far-sighted developer will realize the value in strengthening recollection of two colors, as opposed to broadening it over four. Some of the most renowned and familiar sites rely on a compelling association with a single color.

Contrast

Black text on a white background, the default color scheme of the Web, is high contrast and very readable, ensuring less frustration for visitors with poor eyesight. Maintaining these typical settings across the Web, however, would lead to a particularly bland experience. Additionally, such strong contrast can affect people with overly light-sensitive eyes. A dark text color with an off-white background color can often be more appropriate.

Adequate contrast between your visual elements (text, buttons, images) and their background environments can be achieved with a color scheme that meets the visual goals of your site, whether that is to be exciting and bold, muted and serious, or modern and unique.

Below are a number of examples of text and background color combinations showing poor contrast (left), and sufficient contrast (right). Remember that reading on the Web can be difficult even with a sensibly contrasting set of colors, so please avoid making it any more difficult.

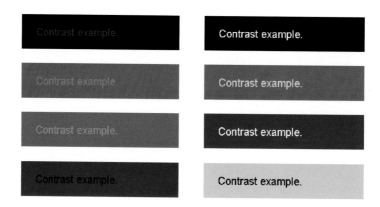

Color Behavior

How colors behave when near each other is an important consideration for any developer. Adjacent complementary or discordant colors can wreak havoc on the eyes of your users, and because of this, care and restraint should be exercised when using such schemes.

If your design does call for text in one color on a background of its complement, then ensure that the contrast between the two is substantial enough to ease legibility. Reading should not be a battle for your audience!

A light block of color near a dark area will appear lighter than it actually is, and the dark one darker. This is a key example of the visual effects colors have on each other through association. In the image below, the two green blocks are the same size and color. This is also true of the charcoal blocks, and in this case it is especially obvious that when surrounded by black, the charcoal block appears lighter than its counterpart on the silver background.

Vision Impairment

The American Foundation for the Blind estimates the number of people who are blind and visually impaired in the United States as 10 million. With similarly significant numbers in Europe, Oceania, and elsewhere, it is important that your color-based decisions do not negatively impact these people.

Color deficiencies commonly associated with partial sight, for example, can make differentiation of hues between colors difficult. It can also impact the ability to discriminate colors with minimal variation in lightness. Discriminating on the basis of saturation (intensity) is difficult for those with congenital color insufficiencies.

Your designs can account for the visually impaired by ensuring that your color choices regarding critical elements (text, buttons, links, and alerts for example) differ significantly with respect to hue, lightness, and saturation.

Examples of poor (left) and sensible (right) combinations are shown below. The more effective examples provide better differentiation between hue and values of lightness and saturation.

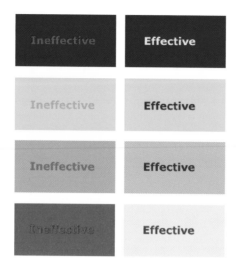

More Resources:

For more information on color behavior and vision impairment as relating to web design, the following are useful resources:

- Customer Experience Solutions: *http://more.btexact.com/ces/colours/othersites.htm*
- Visibone: Color Deficient Vision: *http://www.visibone.com/colorblind/*

Dealing with Bad Corporate Colors

As previously discussed, a developer may encounter a poorly planned logo sporting a couple or group of colors that may generally be best avoided in combination. There are a number of ways in which the effect of these inharmonious colors can be restricted.

One of these methods involves isolating the logo in a block of neutral white or black within your design. If you have created a new scheme around a stronger color from the logo, then the alienated logo will be less likely to conflict with the scheme integrated into the rest of the site.

Confronted by an extremely weak brand, or a brand dominated by a secondary theme (even if it is only a temporary promotion, such as a tropical holiday theme for an airline promoting special packages), a shrewd action would be to de-emphasise or de-saturate of the logo. This allows a featured product, feeling, or sub-brand to gain a higher level of recognition amongst your audience.

Many larger companies rely on the recognition of their brand shape and style, rather than color, to allow sub-schemes to develop for specific markets, products, and promotions. A prime example is Nike, as can be seen demonstrated in the following screenshots.

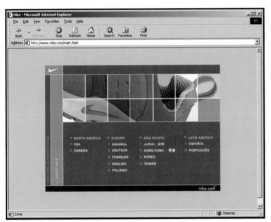

Color Psychology

At the core of color psychology are the near universally accepted conventions of red as warning, and green as progression. It is a good habit to avoid transmitting a mixed message of color and meaning. Coloring an alert pertaining to a successful action or transaction in red is a mixed message. Conversely, a warning titled in green can also be a problem.

With skill, you may be able to adapt these to a similar palette that matches your chosen colors. For example, consistently using a tint of blue to imply success or progress, and an orange to indicate something requiring attention, might be a clever way of maintaining usability and your color palette.

The color selection for your site may also depend on emotional and cultural interpretations. While complete color psychology is out of scope for this resource, there are some basic guidelines that could prove useful.

For example:

- Green is almost universally regarded as a progressive color, signifying growth, energy, the environment and even fertility.

- Black is regarded in many cultures as representing evil or death. It can also, in the right context, suggest sophistication, and is often used for art or jewelry sites.

- White is often simplicity and virtue, but in China, Japan, and the Middle East, it is a color of mourning.

- Yellow, in the Western world, represents caution, sickness and cowardice, but in the East it can stand for honor or prosperity. The right hue or tone of yellow, though, can associate strongly with the sun, and thus can present a bright feel within sites created for children.

- In most regions, red is a strong color indicating danger, passion or anger. In China, it is a sign of luck and festivities.

Differences in color preference between genders may also become a factor in your choice of scheme. From acknowledged studies (Guilford in 1934, Plater in 1967, Kuller in 1976, and Radeloff in 1990) conducted into color preference, some generalizations have been made.

Among these are generalities that men have a higher tolerance for the achromatic neutrals, as well as saturated colors (with a high chromaticity). On the other hand, women have a preference for softer colors.

In tests comparing reaction to red and blue, men have favored the latter, whereas women have fancied red, and while males have liked orange over yellow, females have ranked orange last. Perhaps significantly, there was no substantial difference in inclination towards either light or dark colors.

- *A system of color-preferences, (Guilford, J. P. & Smith, P. C.), The American Journal of Psychology, 73 (4), 487-502.*

- *The Use of Space - Some Physiological and Philosophical Aspects, (Kuller, R.), Paper presented at the Third International Architectural Psychology Conference, University Louis Pasteur, Strasbourg, France.*

- *Role of color in perception of attractiveness, (Radeloff, D. J.), Perceptual and Motor Skills, 71, 151-160.*

- *Reading materials from Color Matters: The Meaning of Color for Gender, (Natalia Khouw) http://www.colormatters.com/khouw.html*

Incorporating Color

While for some, integrating color into a design is innate, for others it is a forced process. Luckily, there are a number of ways in which you can include color within your site. If you have been tasked with brightening or strengthening a site, color will be one more tool in your belt.

Blocks and Backgrounds

Blocks of colors are an instant way to add strength and structure to a design. When using softer colors, they can provide subtle alignment and tie a layout together. Similarly, background colors are the most basic form of color block, and give a site an instant grounding, whether it is an earthy tint, or bold. The primary advantage of areas of uniform color is that they can be rendered using HTML/CSS or, at worst, a single color GIF. They come at a low cost with regard to bandwidth and so are excellent in situations that require a fast-loading web site.

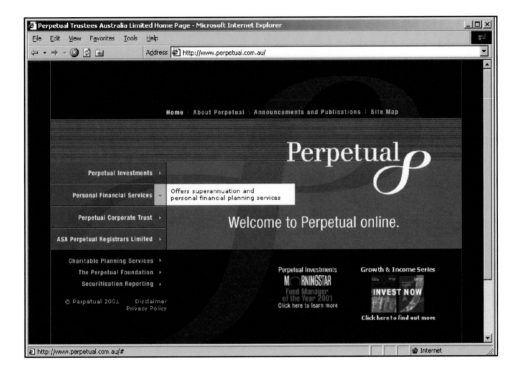

Gradients and Textures

With the addition of a few colors and a gradient or texture, any block of color can be converted into a more tactile region. Gradients, specifically, are often used to provide a transition from one color to a shade or tint of another, or even an analogous hue. They can, however, introduce banding, when the gradient is implemented as a GIF especially. A gradual switch from a hue to its complement is something best avoided, as the central part of the gradient will show the complementary colors negating each other, and leaving gray.

A tiled gradient or texture such as a site background presents opportunities to extend the feeling of your site. For example, using blurs can suggest movement, scratches can create an industrial feel, and earthy textures can step a site away from the usual hard, computer generated lines to something more inline with nature. The following example (*http://www.mdtc.asn.au/*) shows a grass texture in the site header:

While the addition of colors and frequent changes between them increases the file size of textures, they can be easily reduced and exported to either GIF or JPEG formats. As GIFs, they can exist with a reduced palette and maintain a general sharpness of the texture, and as JPEGs, they can be exported at a lower quality to maintain color, but lose definition. See *Chapter 7* for more information on file formats.

Alternating Table Rows

This variation on the standard background as applied to a table is primarily used to present data. The alternating row colors can increase readability - allowing the user to trace their way along a row without accidentally skipping up or down. It is best to select subtle variations that provide substantial contrast with the text within the table.

Links

In times past, developers were heavily encouraged to maintain the standard link colors. As the experience levels of the average Internet user rise somewhat, with sensible choices it is acceptable to adapt your scheme to the status set of link colors: normal, active, visited, and hover. Starting with a bold action-oriented color from your scheme for the normal state is a good start, followed by a visited color that appears faded. Whether this is a shade or a tint of your original hue will depend on the background color being used.

Preserving the underline on your in-text links assists site usability, but within recognizable menu formats, either horizontal or vertical, it is certainly reasonable to remove them, or use some other way to suggest a menu item. Modern browsers support the link:hover attribute, which underlines links as the mouse is rolled over them. Often, this can be enough feedback for users.

It is important to remember, though, that your choice of link color must be a strong and active one. Setting aside one "active" color from your scheme to pertain to actions (links and buttons amongst other elements) is advisable, and it is important to be consistent in its usage.

The *wishlist.com.au* site follows its corporate colors with a gray and orange link scheme. The hover color is orange, default gray, and the visited link color is a darker gray. In this case, the visited links stand out, allow users to easily backtrack and find products previously viewed.

Monochromatic Images

In some situations, colorizing an image with the Adjust Hue/Saturation tool can prove an effective means of strengthening the presence of one color in your design without the distraction of a full color photograph. This is a technique often used within understated designs, such as those for financial companies.

Visual Elements

Applying color to prominent visual elements, such as form submit buttons, image-based navigation, and similar, can give focus to items that lead users through your site. The bright or bold colors of your scheme are usually the best choice for this.

home || design | usability reviews | worksh

A collection of our wri
research including 37s
sites, The 37Better Pr
contingency design wh

Other elements such as borders or dividers are a suitable application of more subtle, accent colors. Slight variations of your central hues (whether tints or shades) should be considered to maintain a harmonious experience. It is also a valid design choice to incorporate strong borders as design elements in their own right, and use them to attract attention to a promotion, for example.

Color Progression

For the most part, color consistency is a web design mantra, but there are situations in which alternative methods may be an option.

The first of these is when using color to designate sections of a site. Department stores frequently use this to provide some sense of separation between men and women's fashion. When implementing this, maintaining consistency through layout and color relationships is essential.

The other is in circumstances where a color theme, or sequential change in opacity (color strength) can indicate progression through a process. This is particularly effective when leading visitors through a check out or user registration process of an online store, for example. It can also be used to indicate depth specifically within a site or breadcrumb trail specifically.

Summary

In this chapter we have introduced the core principles of color theory.

We have covered choosing colors for your site, and thinking about the feeling they will create for your audience. We have also learned that color harmony is an essential part of your site and that you should always be aware of the relationships between the colors you select and work with.

We have also covered how simplicity and consistency can strengthen your message, and with color the situation is little different. Choose colors that support your brand, or otherwise choose colors that support the goals of your site, and apply them consistently.

We have also covered the importance of testing your site to ensure that your colors are well represented on other machines and setups is good practice. Also, we have learned what some colors are telling your users through the innate feelings they create. Keep in mind how colors work together, and consider cultural and generational differences in color perception, and how they might impact your site.

As a final note, be aware of the color schemes in the natural and industrial world around you, and appreciate the inspiration that they can provide. Enjoy the opportunity to experiment with color schemes that you have not previously used.

3

- General typography rules
- When to use images or text
- Coding text with CSS

Author: Adrian Roselli

How to Use Text Effectively - Typography

Now that you've had the opportunity to get a feel for the colors you might want, and what sort of messages they convey to your users, you have think about how you will present the content of the site. After all, why build a site if you don't have anything to say?

All too often the copy on the page is forgotten in the design phase of a project. Sure, typefaces are chosen and assembled in design elements on the page, such as the logo, but what happens to your nice page once you float in a thousand words of toothpick instructions? Will the text have enough contrast? Will the text be large enough? Will the text make your background images look too muddy? Will your design-to-be handle only certain amounts of text?

Of course, not only does your page have to support all the text you insert, but also it has to look good, be easy to read, and make sense. Thankfully, we won't be talking about how to write the content of a site, or edit it, or anything like that. We'll leave that to those guys down in marketing.

In this chapter we'll cover:

- The basics of Typography
- Styling text with Cascading Style Sheets
- When to use images to display text

Typography

The art of typography has existed for as long as there have been printing presses, and to an extent, even before that when scribes would pen passages in great literary works. Johannes Gutenberg is often credited with inventing movable type (creating each letter as a metal blocks and arranging them to form words) in Germany in the 1450s, though there are works from China that date to the thirteenth century. Once the Roman alphabets, with far fewer characters than Chinese, met up with this technique, the technology flourished.

In the last 100 years or so, typography has become more of an art form, owing mostly to the advances in printing presses that allowed control over the layout of printed materials to shift away from the printer to the publisher. Thanks to Linotype and Monotype machines, invented in the 1880s, it became possible to cast blocks of type much more easily. The Linotype machine even allowed a user to enter text on a multi-alphabet keyboard, which was output to a paper tape, which was then fed into the casting machine so it could cast the letters in soft metal. By the 1920s, new typefaces were being designed to take advantage of this level of control and modularity.

Today we refer to the typefaces we choose to use in our essays, web pages, and home-made birthday cards as fonts. A font is just the digital information that makes up a typeface; it refers to the software model of a typeface, but not the typeface itself. It can also mean the physical tape or blocks at a particular size for one typeface, in case you are referring to an old printing press. I will endeavor to use the correct term (typeface) throughout this chapter, as font and typeface really aren't as interchangeable as most people treat them.

I'm going to make you sit through a bit of a lecture now. The rules that follow govern the way text is assembled in all the magazines, newspapers, billboards, and product warning labels that you read. This means you should be able to easily recognize the implementation of some of these rules from your own experiences.

This chapter can only be a basic primer on typography, if you want to learn more, I would recommend picking up a copy of *The Elements of Typographic Style* by Robert Bringhurst, Hartley & Marks, ISBN: 0881791326. It explains everything from the parts of letters to setting rhythm on a printed page with just the text. It's a fascinating read, and it makes for great cocktail party conversations when you can explain a ligature to strangers.

We also need to keep in mind that typography isn't just about cramming letters into a space, but understanding how people read, what moods you can set, and how to use the space that doesn't have any words in it to strengthen your blocks of text.

Parts of a Line

This diagram shows the most basic parts of a line of text, which we'll discuss throughout the chapter. There are more elements that make up an individual letter or line of text, but they don't really matter for much of what we're discussing.

The **capline** is simply the implied horizontal line made from the tops of capital letters. Some letters and many ascenders may extend beyond this line.

The **meanline** indicates the height of lowercase letters, and is usually at the x-height.

The **x-height** is the distance between the baseline and midline of a typeface. Generally this is approximately the height of the lowercase characters that do not have extenders ('o,' 'x,' 'u,' 'z').

The **baseline** is the line on which all the letters rest, rounded letters (o, u) often dent the baseline, pointed letters (v, w) often poke through the baseline, and the feet of most serifs (m,h) sit on the baseline.

The **beardline** is where the bottoms of descenders rest.

The **ascender** and **descender** is the part of a letter that extends above the meanline, or below the baseline. Ascenders often extend above the capline as well. The tall vertical line on a 'd', or the tail of a 'j' are examples of these. They are sometimes called **extenders**.

Other Useful Terms

There are many terms you'll hear when you start to talk to typesetters, printers, graphic designers, typography buffs, and the clinically insane. What follows will give you a basic familiarity with some of the terms that will crop up later in the chapter, and in general discussions of type.

Color

The darkness of the type on the page (or screen) when taken as a whole (or seen from across the room), not its value of red, green, blue, hot pink, or other colors as we know them. The spacing between words, letters, lines, the weight of the typeface, the use of capitals, and even the ink and paper make up the color of the type.

Drop Cap

A large initial capital letter, often much larger than the body copy, and sometimes set with text wrapping around it. You'll see it most often at the beginning of book chapters or magazine articles.

Ems and Ens

For our purposes, type is usually measured in points when you're going to print, or pixels when you're going to display it on the screen. Horizontal spacing, however, is measured in ems. An em is a relative unit, based on the size of the type. In 12-point type, an em is 12 points. Since pixels are not a typographic convention, we'll also work with the idea that it applies to pixels, and in 12-pixel type, an em is 12 pixels. Sometimes you'll hear this pronounced as "mutton" so it isn't confused with the en.

An en is half an em. You can call it a "nut," too, as a counter to the "mutton" of the em. You may also come across some other terms derived from an em. Thin Space, a space measuring a fifth of an em (M/5, although sometimes understood as a sixth of an em in digital typesetting). Mid Space, one quarter of an em, or M/4. Thick Space, a space measuring one third of an em, or M/3

3

Flush

Setting lines of text so that a block of text runs the same length on a side. Flush left text all starts at the same point on the left, flush right text all ends at the same point. Flush left and flush right text is **justified**.

Glyph

A single version of a character. This means the italic version of a letter in one face is a different glyph than its plain version. So 'a' and '*a*' are different glyphs of the same character from the same face.

Gutter

The blank space between columns of text.

Kern

To adjust the spacing between two letters so that the part of one overlaps another, "Tag" is an example where you might want the 'a' to sit under the bar of the 'T'. This also refers to the parts of a letter that extend into the space of another letter.

Lead, Leading

Originally the strip of lead (which is why it rhymes with 'red') between lines of type, in modern times it refers to the space between the baseline of one line of type and the baseline of the next line of type. Lines of type set with no leading are set **solid**.

Pica

Essentially one-sixth of an inch, or equal to 12 points. This unit is traditionally used to measure the length of a line, or the depth of a textblock. The PostScript pica is exactly 1/6 inch, while in traditional measure, it's 0.166 inch or 4.22mm.

Point

If you use just about any word processor that allows you to change type size, you'll note that the sizes are given as points. A point is one twelfth of a pica. This means that there are 72 points in one inch, or 28.5 points in one centimeter. There is a European variation called the Didot point, which comes out to 67.75 per inch, or 26.5 per centimeter. TrueType fonts and most PostScript devices will round the point to exactly 1/72 inch.

Ragged

Lines of text that run different lengths per line, as determined by the words and letters of each line, as opposed to flush or justified

Serif, Sans-serif, Others

For the most part, readers will notice that typefaces come in a few different general flavors. There are the big blocky ones used for headlines in newspapers and on billboards, or other places where the designers want them to be seen with a good deal of prominence. There are the handwriting typefaces, referred to as cursive, that look like someone with extremely good, or sometimes with remarkably poor, penmanship wrote a personal note to the reader.

There are the typefaces that are just bizarre (referred to as fantasy) - letters made of cat heads or something else equally illegible for letters. There are even typefaces with which most of us will be familiar - monospace - where all the letters and spaces are the same width, such as those used in your average text editor (or old-fashioned typewriters).

For the most part, however, you'll only need to concern yourself with the two most general styles of type: serif and sans serif. An example of a serif typeface with which we should all be familiar would be Times New Roman. Simply put, letters with little lines or tails extending out of the ends of the letters are generally serif faces. An example of a sans serif typeface would be Arial. These letters tend to stop where the line ends. No flourishes of ink or tails, just a sturdy edge.

Sans-serif
Arial

Serif
Times New Roman

Monospace
Courier

Traditionally, serif typefaces are preferred for printed blocks of text because the letters come together via the serifs, tails, and other shapes to form a contiguous shape. Most readers recognize shapes of words instead of just reading each letter independently and forming the word in their brains. The entire history of typography points to the benefit of using serif faces in print.

On screen, however, the extra bits and pieces on the letters make serifs harder to read. There aren't as many pixels available, nor are they small enough, to render the sweeping curves of the tail of a lower-case "t", or example. Instead, the letters look blocky and malformed, so sans-serif typefaces are generally the best way to go for on-screen text.

Now, when it comes to using copy on your web pages, you're most likely going to be using one of these two styles of type. When it comes to the images that make up the identity of the site (the logos, banners, and other design elements that use text), it's pretty much up for grabs what you'll use. Some logos use unique typefaces that aren't seen in much use elsewhere, while others just settle for Meta or Myriad and languish in the formality of the letterforms.

Textblock

The box encompassing just the text, or the area that will hold text on a page.

> This is text that is set flush left.
> Sometimes you can have words that are
> way too long to fit on one line neatly.
>
> This is text that is set flush right.
> Sometimes you can have words that are
> way too long to fit on one line neatly.
>
> This is text that is set justified. Sometimes
> you can have words that are way too
> long to fit on one line neatly.

ragged, flush, and justified
within a text block

Weight

The darkness of a typeface, regardless of size; this affects the color of a page.

Word Space

This is the space between words, which is usually fixed for any page with ragged text, but dynamic for text that is justified.

General Typography Rules

Many of the rules I'm going to cover here only apply to when you're setting type in images, primarily because there is still so little control over text on web pages even with CSS. I'm only giving some very general rules, partly because we're only talking about the Web, partly because there are some things that you just cannot do on the Web (with images or without), and partly because some of it may be well beyond the limits of your interest. As I mentioned earlier, there are many wonderful resources out there that address typography. I'd always suggest consulting a book for typography over surfing web sites, primarily because of the nature of the medium: books offer a great opportunity to see type in its natural environment.

Doing the things I suggest below may not prevent hard-core typographers from snickering at you as you toil away on your work, but they'll at least see you're trying, and the results will be more pleasing than making arbitrary decisions.

Remember that the content of the page is usually the most important part of the site. As such, it's a good idea to get a feel for the nature of the text before you start choosing typefaces. Read the content of the page, read the graphical text blocks that you may create, get a feel for the identity of the organization, and choose a typeface appropriate to all of these. The text should also have some relationship not just between the copy and logos, but also with the other design elements on the screen (things like photos, captions, notes, pull-quotes).

Take some time in advance to think about the minor elements of the page, as well. Will the page have a footer with links to disclaimers and copyright information? Will the navigation be text-based or image-based? Will there be special characters used in the copy? The answers to all these help you choose a typeface. Perhaps you need a typeface that has all the extended characters known to man, perhaps you just want one that is legible on the screen and matches your logo.

Clearly if you want to rely on a particular typeface in a project, you need to decide if you will set that type in an image (or even in Flash or SVG), or if you will hope the user has it on his or her system so that it can be called via CSS. Not being able to guarantee a browser has a particular font installed is the bane of type on the Web, and we'll discuss this further later on.

Type Family

Start the project with a single type family. From there, see if you need to include others to handle different types of content, such as headlines, pull-quotes, captions, or anything that can be treated as an exception. Often an extended type family, Lucida for one, can provide enough variations to allow you to still stick with one family throughout. Once you start mixing families, you run the risk of disrupting the harmony of the page or even the image. It doesn't take much to make even the smallest block of text look and feel uncomfortable. If you decide, for example, that your body copy is no good for headers or other heavy duty uses (perhaps it's too light), then find a typeface that is similar in style and structure. This doesn't mean you have to find a clone, or even stick with serif or sans serif. You simply need to find a comfortable match.

When you do mix serif and sans serif typefaces, look to the weight and shape of the letters when making your decision. This includes elements like the x-height of the letters, or the length of descenders. Ideally, you'd like them to be similar. Some examples of a good pairing might be Syntax and Minion, or if you're working from a less robust collection of fonts, faces like Verdana and Trebuchet can match up well if you take care in setting the text. If you find yourself mixing letters from other alphabets, follow the same approach. If you expect you'll need to use many typefaces or match yours to other alphabets, plan this out from the start so there are no surprises. Of course, be certain not to apply too many typefaces to a project, as the end result can range from looking too busy, to appearing like a ransom note.

It's also important to note the familiarity of the typeface. For instance, most viewers will probably find Verdana easier to read on screen, partially because they've seen it so many times that they know the letterforms. On the other hand, using typefaces like Comic Sans can make a web page look very unprofessional, partly because it's a very casual font, and partly because of all the FrontPage-generated home pages that use it.

Established in 1801, Rosencratz & Guildenstern is among the world's oldest and most recognized law firms in intellectual property litigation. Our mission is to provide value to our clients through high-quality service and attention to the smallest detail. To this end, the firm has established a record of excellence and a commitment to the highest ethical standards.

Garamond

Established in 1801, Rosencratz & Guildenstern is among the world's oldest and most recognized law firms in intellectual property litigation. Our mission is to provide value to our clients through high-quality service and attention to the smallest detail. To this end, the firm has established a record of excellence and a commitment to the highest ethical standards.

Verdana

Established in 1801, Rosencratz & Guildenstern is among the world's oldest and most recognized law firms in intellectual property litigation. Our mission is to provide value to our clients through high-quality service and attention to the smallest detail. To this end, the firm has established a record of excellence and a commitment to the highest ethical standards.

Meta-Book Roman

Established in 1801, Rosencratz & Guildenstern is among the world's oldest and most recognized law firms in intellectual property litigation. Our mission is to provide value to our clients through high-quality service and attention to the smallest detail. To this end, the firm has established a record of excellence and a commitment to the highest ethical standards.

Comic Sans

Established in 1801, Rosencratz & Guildenstern is among the world's oldest and most recognized law firms in intellectual property litigation. Our mission is to provide value to our clients through high-quality service and attention to the smallest detail. To this end, the firm has established a record of excellence and a commitment to the highest ethical standards.

Industrial Schizophrenic

Established in 1801, Rosencratz & Guildenstern is among the world's oldest and most recognized law firms in intellectual property litigation. Our mission is to provide value to our clients through high-quality service and attention to the smallest detail. To this end, the firm has established a record of excellence and a commitment to the highest ethical standards.

OCR A Extended

In the examples above, we see some sample copy that might exist on the introduction page of a law firm set in assorted typefaces. The first thing we'll want to do is eliminate the ones that are not even close to a good fit, and then narrow down what's left. We can immediately see that the type set in Comic Sans is too informal for the copy it contains. We can also see the copy in Industrial Schizophrenic is not only hard to read, but it's a busy typeface that doesn't convey the calm professionalism we would want. The OCR A Extended block of copy looks like it belongs on an old computer screen or printout from an old printer, not something that really fits with a law firm. While Verdana is a nice font, its wide letters and letterforms make it look too casual for a law firm. Meta-Book Roman is a wonderful family of typefaces that offers us a lot of options, but the sans serif face doesn't seem formal enough. Also, the color of the type is somewhat dark, making the text look too severe. That leaves us with Garamond. That doesn't mean Garamond wins simply by elimination, however. The serif typeface is much more formal than the others, and its light weight results in an overall color that's light and easy, not oppressive, as we often think of law firms. It also happens to be easier to read on the printed page than any of the other typefaces. Assuming, of course, that we are only going to print. For screen use, it might be worth looking at Georgia, or even Times New Roman, although its on-screen rendering is fairly rough.

Spacing and Kerning

When setting type in images, consider the space between letters, words, and lines of text. If the text is too bunched together, it can not only be hard to read but feel stuffy to a reader, or perhaps convey tension you don't want. Make sure the space between letters gives each letter room to sit on its own without losing itself in the next, while not sitting so far away that the reader has trouble distinguishing words from one another. Generally, the type designer has done a good job of handling letter spacing, so adjusting it is often unnecessary. Kerning, the space between letters, is important between individual pairs of letters. Sometimes an 'o' next to an 'l' just looks too far away, and you have to pull them a little closer so they feel like they are part of the same word. Either way, if you are going to kern letters, be sparing, be consistent, or don't do it at all.

Hello. Ta ta!

loose kerning and letterspacing

Hello. Ta ta!

tight kerning and letterspacing

Hello. Ta ta!

adjusted kerning and letterspacing

The space between words (word spacing) needs to tell the reader where one word ends and another begins, without stringing them across the page so the reader isn't reading in a flow, but by hopping from word to word. The space between lines of text (leading) is also important to help readers move from the end of one line to the beginning of the next without losing their place. Too close, and the reader may reread the same line. Too far, and the reader has to hunt for the next line of text. In the examples below, I've also set the text justified. This means the space between words in every line will be different, so the word spacing is inconsistent. Pay attention to those differences and note which lines of text look too cramped or too open.

This is a block of copy that has undergone some unfortunate leading. It's really rather jumbled and hard to read.	This is a block of copy that has better leading than the others. It's easier to read than either one and looks cleaner.	More copy that has undergone a bit of unfortunate leading. This is more spaced out and is harder to follow from line to line.

This collection of letters and space between letters is referred to as the color of the page. It refers not to the color of ink used, but to the general blackness of the page with type applied. The ultimate goal is to make the color consistent across the entire page. Looking at the above examples, you can see each block of text has a different color to it when compared to the other blocks. Pay attention to how leading, kerning, letter spacing and word spacing all play into that overall color. Keep in mind the design into which you will be inserting this text. It is possible to make an open design very cramped if your text is too dark, or vice versa.

Quantity of Text

The number of words per line is also important for legibility. Generally 45 to 75 characters per line are considered satisfactory for a single-column page. 66 characters are often considered ideal, however, with users able to control their own window sizes or font settings, it's hard to know what the user may see. You can be almost certain that it won't be what you see. This issue has also plagued liquid designs - page designs where the content and design expand and contract to fill the user's window - by rendering lines of text far longer than the recommended maximum. There is some debate amongst site designers on various web development forums about whether or not liquid designs should include the copy of the page as well.

Choosing to center your page content, make it left-aligned (ragged right), right-aligned (ragged left) or justified (left- and right-aligned) is a challenge many designers face. For the most part, left-aligned (like this paragraph) will be your best bet until setting justified text becomes something browsers can do well. There is also a cultural reason why it is easier to read text that has a fixed left-alignment - English is written from the left to the right.

Justified text (like this paragraph) can look very blocky, giving the page a squared-off appearance. While this kind of thing is fine for some designs, paragraph after paragraph of fully justified text can appear daunting. There is no way in for the reader, and having the lines of the same length means that the eye makes many more repetitive movements, which could easily lead to strain. Too many browsers (and word processors) make poor decisions on how to handle the word spacing needed to extend the content to   the   edge   of   the   paragraph.

Right-aligned (like this paragraph) should only be used when there is a very good reason stemming from the design of the page, as readers have a harder time coming back to the next line after reading a line of text. Particularly when the next line is short.

Centered text is right out, because it looks terrible. The copy on a page should never be centered without very good reasons (like parody, or poetry).

Manipulating Letters

Once you're in an illustration or photo manipulation package like Macromedia FreeHand or Adobe Photoshop, you may have the urge to start stretching or squishing letters. Typefaces don't like that. It's certainly a shortcut to fit a block of text into a tiny space in your design, but you have to resist the urge, barring some very good reasons (such as cramming a couple of extra letters into an existing design over which you have no control). A typeface has usually been designed to be legible unchanged. Adjusting the shape of the letterform may not only impede readability, but it may even change the mood of the text.

> A normal block of text.
>
> A squished block of text.
>
> A stretched block of text, but only a little.

Separating Text

Many readers here are familiar with a de facto standard on the Web that says all paragraphs must be separated from one another by a full blank line. This is fine. It is also possible, however, to indent or outdent the start of a new paragraph using a number of techniques (such as CSS, non-breaking spaces, and spacer images, although CSS will prove to be more forward-compatible and result in less code bloat). If you do this, keep in mind that opening paragraphs and the paragraphs after headers and subheads need not be indented. If you do indent or outdent, make sure the length of the indent or outdent isn't so long that it breaks up the flow of the page. Usually a few characters is sufficient, or one or two ems.

When dealing with large blocks of quotations, something that would usually sit within a `<blockquote>` element, you may wish to add a little extra space above and below the quotation in your CSS. If quoting verse (poems, limericks, lyrics), make sure the quotation is indented from the rest of the copy on the page.

Abbreviations

When setting abbreviations or acronyms in your text, use what are called small caps if available in the typeface you've chosen. They look very much like the capital letters of a typeface, except smaller. They are different from the capitals of a typeface in their weight and proportions (along with other minor differences). If you don't have small caps, you can approximate them by setting the size of the capitals in question to smaller than normal, ideally matching the x-height (the height of the lowercase letter 'x') of the rest of the text in the page. We'll see an example of this later on with CSS.

Ligatures

Sometimes letters are so close to one another that they seem to combine. These combinations of letters are called ligatures. The ones with which you may be most familiar are the 'œ,' as in hors d'œuvre, or 'æ,' as in encyclopædia. There are many other ligatures out there, but these are the most common. If you think you may encounter these in your content, be certain your typeface has the characters available, and if you are using CSS to define a series of fonts, be certain to check all the faces in that collection.

Emphasis

When setting content apart on the page, for example when you want to emphasize or stress a particular word or phrase in your copy, only change one parameter at a time. Make the text either bold or italic, for example, but not both. You can even use small caps, but you should reserve that for when you know you have absolute control over the text, such as in a graphic.

Underlines

Avoid using underlines. On the Web underlines imply a hyperlink. Most rules for the use of underlines stem from a time when typewriters were the only method people had to produce text that wasn't hand-written. Now we can go back to using italics and bold appropriately, since computers aren't as restricted as typewriters.

Headings

Page headings and subheads (`<h1>` through `<h6>`) need not be extremely large. Often, setting them the same size as the type on the page works for many designs. This helps preserve the consistent color of the page. If you want very large headings, consider making them a light gray or other light color (assuming you're on a white page background) to help reduce the weight they have on the page. Keep in mind, however, the value of having page headings of different sizes (or with different indenting, for example) to indicate to the reader that there is some sort of hierarchy. This is one of those fine lines we have to walk when designing the page, but ultimately, with CSS you can still maintain good document structure and make it look as you see fit.

Images versus Text

So you've figured out what typefaces you want to use, and you think you're ready to start stuffing them into words. Before you do that, you need to decide if that headline is going to be inserted as an image, or if it's going to be drawn by the browser and CSS. It's often tempting to use an image, so that you can guarantee your users will see your chosen typeface in all its glory, but there are some considerations you need to weigh up before you make that decision.

The first thing you need to consider is how the image will be used. Is it navigation, a header, body copy, a pull quote, a footer, or something else? How important is it that the typeface be maintained in that context? Consider the following issues when choosing to use an image for text:

- Maintainability
- Localization
- Content Management Systems
- Accessibility
- Identity
- Printing

Maintainability

If you choose to use images in place of text, every time you need to change a line of text, fix a spelling error, or even adjust things like color or weight, you have to edit the image. Often, this means opening the source file in an application such as Photoshop, making the necessary changes, and then exporting the image into the desired format.

If you need to rely on outside staff, lower-level staff, or anyone who might not be conversant with the software, then you've increased the time and difficulty necessary to change a block of text, which increases the cost of maintaining the site overall.

The frequency with which text will need to be changed is a good indicator of whether or not it is worthwhile. If the copy will never be changed, maintainability is no longer a concern. If the image will be changed every day or week, then it will be an issue. This depends, however, on each project and whether or not daily/weekly/monthly is considered frequent when it comes to determining the costs involved.

Localization

Let's say you're working on a site about animals, and one of the navigation items for the site is "Aardvark". In English, that word is only eight characters long, and when you crop the image down to so that it's a tight fit, you won't have much room to handle longer words when you translate it. In Spanish, the best word might be "Oso hormiguero", which is a full six characters longer. Without either adjusting the size of the type, or the width of the characters, the Spanish translation won't fit into the space allotted for the English version of the word.

Many other languages can result in longer words than that, as well. As such, you need to consider this localization bloat if your site has an audience, now or in the future, that speaks more than your native tongue. In such instances, text is much easier to change than images.

Content Management Systems

If you're designing a site to be powered by a content management system (CMS), then you need to determine what that CMS can affect. Does it create the navigation dynamically? What about the headings and subheadings? Footer information? If it does, using images to drive any of these will be pretty much impossible, or at least render the CMS unable to do its day-to-day job by tying up valuable processing power. Granted, your average CMS allows you to create a template that can either accept content from the CMS, or use hard-coded HTML, but it's generally best not to remove features from a system just to control the typeface of a site.

Accessibility

Don't forget that not all of your audience may be as sharp-eyed as you are. Clearly, one concern is users who are blind. If you use images, as long as you include appropriate text in your alt attributes, you should be fine. If you use text rather than images, then you're still in good shape for addressing users who are blind browsing with a text reader.

For users with vision impairments, it's not quite as easy a fix. These users can still see the page, just not as well as you or I. They may be colorblind, have low vision, difficulty seeing detail, color, or even suffer eyestrain while reading the page. You need to ensure the images and text you create are large enough to be seen, have enough contrast against the background, and don't use colors that, when paired, can make the text invisible or hard to see for users who are colorblind.

Just as many sites now offer style switchers to let users choose between color schemes, many are also offering the ability to size text as well. If the site is coded with relative units in the CSS, then the users can even do it themselves. If the site you are building has an audience that may wish to scale text up and down, then you should consider this as an accessibility issue.

And let's not forget search engines. Search engines prefer plain text and structural markup when it comes to weighing the content of a page. If all your copy or keywords are hidden in images, then the search engine spider cannot get to them. alt attributes can certainly help, but they usually don't carry the weight plain text does to a search engine spider.

It's worth noting that accessibility also applies to how quickly the page downloads for your reader. If the page has all copy in images, even with the best alt attributes, it can still take quite a while for all the images of text to download. If your users have a particularly slow connection, this can drive them away from your site.

And finally, consider the impact on cutting and pasting. There are many users on the Web who go straight to the contact page of a site and copy the address only to paste it into their word processor as the head of a letter or to address an envelope. All too often, text is hidden in images so that it cannot be easily copied off the page.

Identity

Is the format for the copy, text or images, appropriate to maintain the identity of the project? Sometimes you absolutely have to use the Caslon or Bodoni typefaces in a subhead or as a product title or hiding in a corner of the screen. In these cases, as long as you've addressed the issues above, you should be in a good position to make sure the use of the image as text isn't frivolous, and if it is, is at least backed up with sound reasoning to make it work the best you can.

Printing

Let's not forget that some people like to print the page on screen and take it with them somewhere - perhaps even a meeting where they want to show off your client list and maybe even hire you. Anyway, imagine how all your text anti-aliased to your background color will look when printed with the color halos (assuming it's not white text) at 72dpi. It can get pretty ugly and illegible. Print stylesheets via CSS can also make your wonderfully colorful text mellow out to a sardonic black for easy printing, something you can't do with an image. A brief introduction to print stylesheets can be found at: *http://www.evolt.org/article/nondes/20/22225/index.html*

Coding Text

Once you've finally nailed down the parts of your page that will hold good old-fashioned text, you need to figure out the best way to code it. Since this book is a focused on design, I won't go too far into the HTML necessary to mark up the content of your pages, but I do need to address enough of it so you know how we'll apply the CSS a little further on.

Screen-Friendly Fonts

Some time ago Microsoft released a collection of fonts that were specifically designed for on-screen viewing. Using a few well-regarded typographers they created a free collection of fonts that were distributed with Internet Explorer and MS Office, and later installed in the operating system or available for independent download. Most users of Internet Explorer 4.0 or later, or Windows 98 or later, have these fonts on their system. This includes Macintosh and even some UNIX users as well. It's worth noting that Microsoft recently started charging for new downloads of this collection, so these fonts may now become less common on non-Windows platforms. Samples of these fonts are shown below:

Trebuchet MS
Trebuchet MS Bold
Trebuchet MS Italic
Trebuchet MS Bold Italic

Georgia
Georgia Bold
Georgia Italic
Georgia Bold Italic

Verdana
Verdana Bold
Verdana Italic
Verdana Bold Italic

There are many other fonts out there that are optimized for screen viewing, including "pixel" fonts, which are designed for screen only, and usually for very small sizes.

In general it's a good idea to find a font that displays well on screen, whether it will be used in an image, or rendered as HTML. If the user doesn't have the font that we designed our page in, their viewing experience will be impaired; worse, the site might not be displayed properly.

HTML

For the scope of this chapter, I will be showing code samples in HTML 4.01 Transitional. I do this not because I don't believe in XHTML, but because I believe the average web site will be using HTML 4.01 for a while to come, and because the syntax is so similar to XHTML 1.0 Transitional that this shouldn't be too hard for readers to convert in their mind. Most of these elements will work in the strict versions of HTML 4.01 and XHTML 1.0 and 1.1 (and even in XHTML 2.0), but we'll leave it to the reader to decide which is the standard they wish to use.

Elements for Marking Up Text

HTML 4.01 has far fewer tags than you might think. Most of them, however, have something to do with marking up text. You can see the complete list of elements in HTML 4.01, along with links to their appropriate use, at the World Wide Web Consortium (W3C) site at: *http://www.w3.org/TR/html401/index/elements.html.*

For the benefit of the reader, I'm going to list some of the more common ones here to save you having to actually sit in front of a computer now I've managed to get you away from one for a little while. There are more than are listed here, but this will get you started.

Element	Description
`<a>`	This is an anchor element, usually used to hold hyperlinks, as `<a href="">`, but also used for marking a place on the page for an in-page hyperlink or anchor.
`<abbr>`	Holds abbreviations. Paired with a `title` attribute, it can help tell users what an abbreviation stands for. Sadly, Microsoft Internet Explorer doesn't render styles for `<abbr>`. The general consensus is to use `<acronym>` until `<abbr>` is supported when targeting IE users.
`<acronym>`	Holds acronyms. Like `<abbr>`, when paired with a `title` attribute, it can help tell users what an acronym means.
`<b>`	Styles the text within as bold. Has no other meaning or use other than to make the text look heavy. Use `<strong>` in favor of `<b>` as it implies semantic meaning
`<big>`	Tells the browser to use a "big" font. Generally, using CSS is a much better alternative. Opposite of (you guessed it) `<small>`.
`<blockquote>`	Designed to hold long quoted passages. This is block level, unlike its inline cousin, the `<q>`.
` `	Acts as a single line break.
`<cite>`	Citation to other sources often used with a title attribute to reference the source.
`<code>`	Holds a chunk of programming code to be displayed. By default, it's generally endered in a monospace font. Essentially the inline equivalent of `<pre>`.
`<dd>`	Definition description. Used with `<dt>` and `<dl>`.
`<dl>`	Definition list. Holds a collection of phrases or words, and their definitions. Used with `<dt>` and `<dd>`.
`<dt>`	Definition title. Used with `<dd>` and `<dl>`.
`<em>`	Text to be emphasized. Usually rendered as italic by visual browsers, to be spoken with emphasis by text-to-speech browsers. Use `<em>` in favor of `<i>` as it implies semantic meaning.
`<font>`	This is a deprecated tag that can and should be avoided if possible. Use CSS to set the font face, color, and size of text.
`<h1>`,`<h2>`,`<h3>`, `<h4>`,`<h5>`,`<h6>`	Headings and subheadings. Generally rendered in bold with decreasing size as you climb the numbers.
`<i>`	Renders text as italic. Has no meaning or use other than setting text in italics. Use `<em>` in favor of `<i>` as it implies semantic meaning.

Table continued on following page

How to Use Text Effectively - Typography

3

Element	Description
`<label>`	Linked with a form field (by the `'for'` attribute to the form element's `'id'` attribute), this tells the browser that a particular block of text belongs to a particular form element.
`<li>`	An individual list item. Used in `<ol>` and `<ul>` lists.
`<ol>`	An ordered list. Can be rendered with numbers, letters, Roman numerals, or a mix
`<p>`	The paragraph tag. Holds each paragraph of generic body copy.
`<pre>`	Holds preformatted text, retaining line breaks and spacing. Generally used to render blocks of computer code, and usually rendered in a monospace font. Handy for tacky ASCII art, too. Essentially the block-level equivalent of `<code>`.
`<q>`	The inline cousin to the `<blockquote>`, it holds small chunks of quoted text. The W3C specifications request that browsers automatically insert quotes around any copy in a `<q>`. Mozilla now does this, so it's worth considering leaving quote marks off this text and styling with color or italic text to set it apart for users on older browsers (look closely at my later screen capture and you'll see extra quotes around the quote in Netscape 7).
`<small>`	The inverse to the `<big>` element, it tells the browser to render the text in a "small" font. Generally, using CSS is a much better alternative.
`<strong>`	Text to be treated strongly, or with strong emphasis. Usually rendered as bold by visual browsers, to be spoken with emphasis by text-to-speech browsers. Use `<strong>` in favor of `<b>` as it implies semantic meaning.
`<sub>`	Subscript text.
`<suq>`	Superscript text.
`<ul>`	Unordered list, generally using plain bullets of discs, circles, and squares.

Now let's see these in action. Say we have a generic page with generic page content on it. OK, I'm lying, we don't. So let's make one. We're going to work in many of the HTML elements above so we can see how it looks.

The sample code:

```
<!DOCTYPE HTML PUBLIC "-//W3C//DTD HTML 4.01 Transitional//EN">

<html>
<head>
<title>Test Page</title>
<meta http-equiv="Content-Type" content="text/html; charset=iso-8859-1">
</head>
<body>
<h1>This is a heading 1, or &lt;h1&gt;</h1>
```

```
<p>
Opening paragraph with a <a href="foo.html">hyperlink</a> that goes somewhere. Now
let's insert an abbreviation for <abbr title="World Wide Web Consortium">W3C</abbr>
and an acronym for <acronym title="Document Object Model">DOM</acronym>.
</p>

<p>
I only use superscript when talking about things like the 1<sup>st</sup> of the
month, and subscript when talking about chemistry, like H<sub>2</sub>O.
</p>

<h2>This is a heading 2, or &lt;h2&gt;</h2>

<p>
<strong>Here is some text that is strong</strong> and <em>here is some text with
emphasis</em>.<br>
Similarly, <b>here is some bold text</b> and <i>some italic text</i>
</p>

<h3>This is a heading 3, or &lt;h3&gt;</h3>

<p>
Here we have an inline quote, <q title="Author unknown">&quot;I am not wearing any
pants.&quot;</q> We lifted it from a magazine article titled <cite title="From Pants
Weekly">Where Are My Pants?</cite>.
</p>

<blockquote>
This is copy quoted from another source, and much too long to display inline with
the rest of the paragraph.
</blockquote>

<h4>This is a heading 4, or &lt;h4&gt;</h4>

<p>
The code in this paragraph uses the <code>&lt;code&gt;&lt;/code&gt;</code> tags.
</p>

<pre>
It could also sit in a &lt;pre&gt;.
  But that wouldn't make sense
  since it is very short and can
  be referenced inline.
  Ok, end of &lt;pre&gt;.
</pre>

<h5>This is a heading 5, or &lt;h5&gt;</h5>
<ul>
 <li>This is the first item in an unordered list.</li>
 <li>This is second.</li>
 <li>It uses the &lt;ul&gt; and &lt;li&gt; elements.
  <ol>
    <li>And this is the first item in a nested ordered list.</li>
    <li>This is second in the nested list.</li>
    <li>It uses the &lt;ol&gt; and &lt;li&gt; elements.</li>
```

```
    </ol>

  </li>
</ul>

<h6>This is a heading 6, or &lt;h6&gt;</h6>

<dl>
 <dt>This is the title of the definition</dt>
 <dd>And this is the definition in our definition list.</dd>
 <dt>Another phrase to be defined.</dt>
 <dd>Another nebulous definition.</dd>
</dl>

</body>
</html>
```

Now, without CSS we can expect it to look like the following:

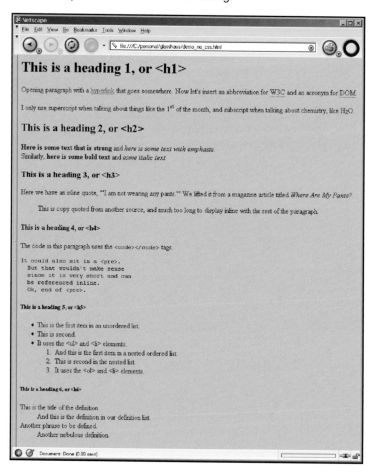

Looks kinda boring, huh? Well, it is. It's just markup without any style other than the limited styles that some of the tags imply. So now we've got to look at applying some of the typography rules we've learned above with CSS to make it a little bit more exciting.

Cascading Style Sheets (CSS)

There is a whole lot of detail we could go into here on what CSS can and can't do, where it can go, all the discussions of appropriate use, browser support, and wonky behavior, but we're going to defer to CSS books on that one. We'll address some of this here, but only as it applies to type. You can get a good primer on CSS with a copy of *Cascading Style Sheets, Separating Content from Presentation*, glasshaus, ISBN: 1904151043. It will look like this one - all blue on the outside, and full of meaty goodness.

CSS offers us a lot of ability to play with the styles of type, and much like the HTML chart above, I'll present an abbreviated CSS chart here, followed by a sample of how to apply it to the HTML page above. When we're done, you should have an idea of how easy it can be to make that boring text do something other than sit there waiting for the next train to Dullsville.

I'm going to show you mostly CSS1 properties, with the CSS2 addition of the 'inherit' value to many of them. Many of the CSS2 properties aren't widely supported. You can read up on the CSS specifications on the W3C site at: *http://www.w3.org/TR/REC-CSS1* (for CSS1), and *http://www.w3.org/TR/REC-CSS2/* (for CSS2).

Property	Values	Description
font-family	The name of a typeface, or the generic keyword for serif, sans-serif, cursive, fantasy, or monospace	A prioritized list of fonts. Fonts listed first are used first, and in the absence of that font, the browser moves down the list until it finds one that matches.
font-style	normal, italic, oblique	Used to select an italic or oblique face from a font, if one is available. If not, the browser will approximate it.
font-varient	normal, small-caps	Allows you to set a block of text to display as small caps, and if a small caps version of the font is not available, the browser will approximate it.
font-weight	normal, bold, bolder, lighter, 100, 200, 300, 400, 500, 600, 700, 800, 900	Allows you to set text as bold, or bolder or lighter than its parent. Each number represents darker text, with 400 equal to normal weight, and 700 equal to bold. This only works if the font has the ability to scale to those weights, otherwise in practice you are limited to 'normal' and 'bold.'

Table continued on following page

How to Use Text Effectively - Typography

Property	Values	Description
font-size	This can be made up of keywords (xx-small, x-small, small, medium, large, x-large, xx-large; larger, smaller), units, or percent	Sets the size of the text. This can set a specific size, or set it in relation to styles applied to its parent.
background	This can accept images, colors, and other values that can modify images	Sets a background color or image on an element
color	Made up of any valid CSS color value, including traditional hex colors	Sets the color of the text or foreground element.
word-spacing	Accepts normal, inherit, or a unit measurement	Adjusts space between words, accepting both positive and negative values.
letter-spacing	Accepts normal, inherit, or a unit measurement	Adjusts space between letters, accepting both positive and negative values.
text-decoration	none, underline, overline, line-through, blink, inherit	Adjusts lines under, through, and above text. Also has a blink style, although I suggest you ignore it.
vertical-align	baseline, sub, super, top, text-top, middle, bottom, text-bottom, or a percentage measurement	Can set text above or below the baseline, and also handles superscript and subscript.
text-transform	capitalize, uppercase, lowercase, none, inherit	Capitalizes the first letter of each word, the entire block of text, shifts it all to lowercase, or overrides any styles from the parent.
text-align	left, right, center, justify, inherit (In CSS2, can accept a string for aligning the content of table cells, such as aligning on a decimal or particular character)	Sets text to left or right aligned, centers it, or justifies it
text-indent	Accepts length or percent units. Also accepts the keyword inherit	Creates an indent (or outdent if a negative value) on the first line of a block of text.
Line-height	Accepts units, numbers, percentages, or the keyword normal to override parent styles	Equivalent to leading in that it sets the height of the styled line of text, independent of the size of the type, but does not accept negative values.

Property	Values	Description
Margin	Length or percent units	Adjusts the space outside a block-level container
padding	Length or percent units	Adjusts the space inside a block-level container
border	Shorthand property for setting border colors, size, and style	Used to define a border in one go. You can also define each part individually using: `border-color`, `border-width`, `border-style`
white-space	`normal`, `pre`, `nowrap`, `inherit`	Allows you to mimic the effects of a `<pre>` tag, or keep lines of text from wrapping.
list-style-type	`disc`, `circle`, `square`, `decimal`, `lower-roman`, `upper-roman`, `lower-alpha`, `upper-alpha`, `none`	Used to set the style of bullet used in a list
list-style-image	A URL to an image, or the keyword `none` to set it to nothing	Allows you to use an image in place of a bullet. If the image is not found, it will default to the bullet style specified.
list-style-position	`inside`, `outside`	Determines if the bullet for the list is drawn inside the block of items, or outside

You'll note that some of the CSS properties above refer to a "parent". This is simply the container that holds the element we're looking at. So, in our HTML example, `<strong>` is a child of `<p>`, which is a child of `<body>`, and `<body>` is a parent of `<p>`, which is a parent of `<strong>`.

Applying CSS

So let's take some of the styles above and apply them to our sample HTML document and see what we can come up with. Granted, the application of CSS here will be gratuitous, so it may not be the prettiest thing you've seen.

The first thing we'll want to do is adjust the background color and then choose a basic typeface and other styles for the page. So, in our `<head></head>`, we'll add a `<style></style>` block, although we could call out to a linked file or import a file. Linking to an external file (or otherwise importing it) is generally the best way to go, as you can maintain all the styles for a site in one file, and the CSS file only needs to be downloaded to the browser cache once. At that point, styles in the `<head></head>` will generally only exist to override styles in your external sheets. For now we'll create the styles in the document itself using the following code:

```
<style type="text/css">
<!--
body
    { background-color : #ffffff ;
    color : #000000 ;
    font-size : 12px ;
    font-family : Verdana, Geneva, Arial, Helvetica, sans-serif ;
    line-height : 140% ; }
-->
</style>
```

You'll note I listed Geneva before Arial. This is because it is more legible on-screen than Helvetica, so we tell the browser to use Verdana first, then Geneva if it doesn't have our first choice, then Arial, then Helvetica, and finally any sans serif font it has. Since not many users on Windows will have Geneva (or rather not many users on Windows won't have Verdana, which will be used in preference to Geneva if the browser has access to it), users on Macintosh systems will be presented with a screen font that is legible - if they don't have Verdana. It should be noted that if a font has spaces in its name, then it should be enclosed in quotes, for example: `font-family: "Industrial Schizophrenic";`

You can also use fonts that are on your system, but you should keep in mind the likelihood that a user won't have them. Just because I have Industrial Schizophrenic on my system doesn't mean my users will, so I should be sure I specify enough fonts that they'll see at least something similar to what I want. I should also be sure that my design doesn't rely on a specific font called in my CSS, since that could prove to be a little odd-looking when the page is rendered with something completely different.

It's worth mentioning that 'line-height' is one of the properties renowned for giving Netscape Navigator versions 4.x problems. Often, text starts to overflow and sit on top of images, or just get lost on the page. Navigator 4.x also has problems with 'padding' and 'margin' properties on a page.

As a brief aside, it is possible to exclude styles from Navigator without relying on often buggy client-side script, or server-side scripts that can detect the wrong browser if not well-coded. Navigator does not understand the `@import` property of CSS, but more standards-compliant browsers do. Using this deficiency in Navigator, you can create a CSS file that contains all your margin, line-height, and padding properties (and any other styles that give you trouble in Navigator) that will never be seen by Navigator simply by calling it via `@import`. You can even override styles you've inserted in your main CSS file just for Navigator by restyling them in your imported CSS file, but you must call that file after your main CSS file in the sourcecode. Below is an example of calling both CSS files in a page, and would go in the `<head></head>` of your HTML.

```
<link rel="stylesheet" type="text/css" href="/master.css">
<style type="text/css">
<!--
        @import "/extras.css";
-->
</style>
```

You should also note that I chose pixels as the unit for my type size (12px). Internet Explorer 5+ for Windows seems to be the only browser that cannot natively scale pixel units based on user preferences, and given its large market share, it effectively makes pixel units unfriendly for those who need to see the copy on a site larger than it was designed.

You can avoid this problem with relative units, like em, or by using percentages, although both can cause rendering inconsistencies, and percentages tend to cause developers more trouble than anything. You can also use the keywords (large, small, etc.), but they too tend to be rendered inconsistently. The final option is to skip specifying a size at all, and let it be driven by the browser's default settings.

Now that we've got the basic style down for the page, let's start to style the individual elements.

I don't know about you, but I find a subhead that's smaller than the body copy seems kind of silly, so the first thing I want to do is ensure no subheads are smaller than my copy. Since I don't want my `<h1>`s to be larger than a melon, I'll explore using indentation along with type size to still convey some visual hierarchy. I also want to add some color as well, to make it a little more interesting. Just make sure all these new styles we're making get inserted before the closing `</style>` tag. I've also added a couple of unnecessary styles (letter-spacing and font-variant) to `<h1>` and `<h2>` just to see how they might look:

```
h1   {   font-size : 160% ;
     font-weight : bold ;
     color : #009900 ;
     font-variant : small-caps ; }

h2   {   font-size : 140% ;
     font-weight : bold ;
     color : #009900 ;
     letter-spacing : 10px ; }

h3   {   font-size : 120% ;
     font-weight : bold ;
     color : #009900 ; }

h4   {   font-size : 100% ;
     font-weight : bold ;
     color : #009900 ; }

h5   {   font-size : 100% ;
     font-weight : bold ;
     text-indent : 3em ;
     color : #009900 ; }

h6   {   font-size : 100% ;
     font-weight : bold ;
     text-indent : 6em ;
     color : #009900 ; }
```

From here, I'd consider styling the elements that already have implicit styles. Use the CSS to reinforce those, and then maybe add a little more on. Bold and italic text are good samples for us, along with a few other styles:

```
i, em, cite {  font-style : italic ;}

b, strong {  font-weight : bold ; }

sup {  vertical-align : super ;
    font-size : 80% ; }

sub {  vertical-align : sub ;
    font-size : 80% ; }

small {  font-size : 75% ; }

big {  font-size : 125% ; }
```

Finally, let's take advantage of CSS to emphasize some elements which otherwise might be missed by the reader:

```
abbr, acronym {  border-bottom : 1px dotted #cc0000 ; }

code {  font-family : Courier New, Courier, monospace ;
    color : #000066 ; }

pre {  font-family : Courier New, Courier, monospace ;
    color : #000066 ;
    white-space : pre ;
    background-color : #cccccc ; }

blockquote {  font-style : italic ;
    margin : 5px ;
    padding : 5px ;
    background-color : #eeeeee ; }

a:link {  color : #0000cc ;
    text-decoration : underline ; }

dd {  text-indent : -1em ; }

ul {  list-style-type : square ; }

ol {  list-style-type : upper-alpha ; }
```

Now, we shouldn't expect a work of art from our page, but it should look a lot less boring, right? Well, let's have a look at our sample:

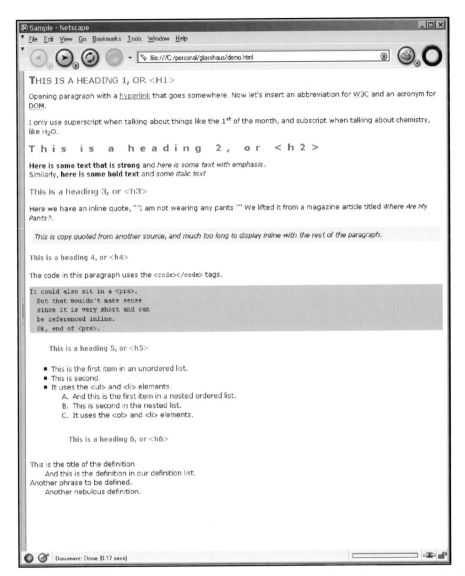

All of the differences you see above came only from the use of the CSS file. Compare that with the original raw HTML page.

Other Methods to Apply Styles

Up until now we've only talked about applying styles to elements that already exist. What happens if you have a paragraph that, for some reason, you don't want to look like other paragraphs? Well, there are a few ways we can address this, using selectors in CSS. Again, since going in-depth into CSS is beyond the scope of this book, I'll direct you to the W3C specifications, and the CSS book referenced previously for more detail. We'll only address a few of the more common selectors here.

If we have a paragraph that we want to look different from all the others, then we need to find some way to identify it. Let's say that we want a particular paragraph to have a background color of blue. These are some different ways we can single it out on the page.

Classes

If we assign the `<p>` tag a class of `"blue"`, like this:

```
<p class="blue">
```

we can use the following CSS to select it and style it:

```
.blue   {   background-color : #0000ff ; }
```

Since there can be many elements on a page with that class, we can make it very specific by only affecting `<p>` tags, and not any other elements with that class:

```
p.blue   {   background-color : #0000ff ; }
```

The sample above will cause you some consternation if you are coding it for Netscape 4.x. Instead of coloring the whole block of the `<p>` blue, it will only color the background of each letter, making it look pretty rough. One way around this, and a bit of a hack, is to stuff the `<p>` in a `<div>` and style the `<div>`. It's up to you to determine the need to support Navigator 4.x in cases like this.

IDs

Much the same way we set a class, we can set an ID. An ID can only exist once per page, so we generally don't need to get so specific as we needed to with classes above (by adding the element we wish to affect). It is allowed, however, and can often make the code more readable when you see the element you are styling immediately preceding the ID value. The CSS, including the more specific selector:

```
#blue   {   background-color : #0000ff ; }
p#blue   {   background-color : #0000ff ; }
```

And the HTML would look like this:

```
<p id="blue">
```

Children

If your paragraph sits within a `<div>`, or other container, you can select it that way as well:

```
div > p {  background-color : #0000ff ; }
```

The first element before the greater-than sign is the parent and the second is the child. You can also mix and match some of the selects above. For example, let's say you have the following:

```
<div id="foot">
<p class="blue">hi.</p>
</div>
```

You can select the `<p>` any one of the following ways:

```
div#foot > p {  background-color : #0000ff ; }
#foot > p {  background-color : #0000ff ; }
#foot > p.blue {  background-color : #0000ff ; }
div#foot > p.blue {  background-color : #0000ff ; }
```

There are other ways you can select it, as well. You simply need to decide which is the most simple and the most robust for your needs.

Descendants

Sometimes the element you want is nested even further. Let's say we want the `<strong>` in the `<p>` which is in the `<div>`:

```
<div id="foot">
<p><strong>hi</strong> there.</p>
</div>
```

Since the `<strong>` isn't a child of the `<div>`, but is a child of the `<p>`, which is a child of the `<div>`, we know the `<strong>` is a descendant. It's very much like the code for selecting children, but without the greater-than sign:

```
#foot strong {  background-color : #0000ff ; }
```

As with children above, you can select the `<strong>` in a variety of different ways:

```
div#foot strong {  background-color : #0000ff ; }
#foot p strong {  background-color : #0000ff ; }
#foot > p > strong {  background-color : #0000ff ; }
#foot p > strong {  background-color : #0000ff ; }
div#foot > p strong {  background-color : #0000ff ; }
```

Hyperlinks

You can also use CSS to adjust the style of a hyperlink in different states. The selectors are:

Selector	Description
a:link	Styles the hyperlink when it has not yet been visited.
a:visited	Styles the hyperlink when it has been visited.
a:hover	Styles the hyperlink while the mouse pointer is over the link. This style will not work in Navigator 4.x.
a:active	Styles the hyperlink while the mouse button is pressed.

These can be integrated with the other selectors discussed above so that, rather than affect all links, they only affect those within the selection we desire. For example:

```
<div id="foot">
<p><a href="foo.html">go there</a> now.</p>
</div>
```

could be styled by:

```
#foot a:link  {  text-decoration : underline ; }
```

Summary

Ideally, at the end of this chapter you should have not only a basic understanding of what makes up good typography, but the ability to use HTML and CSS to integrate some of this into your page, as well as the understanding to apply it to your image editor of choice.

We have seen a little about what makes up a letter, and what happens when we get lots of words together in a paragraph. We have discussed the pros and cons of using images instead of text (it should be kept to a minimum). We looked at an example of how we can use CSS to specify how we want our text to appear in the browser.

How to Use Text Effectively - Typography

4

- **Types of visual element**
- **Styles to try**

Author: Isaac Forman

Visual Elements

Introduction

While not everyone possesses a talent for design, with an understanding of some key guidelines and principles, anyone can improve their ability to develop web materials. Keeping your templates simple, maintaining a color scheme, and ensuring consistency with regular headers and footers are all very straightforward building blocks for your sites. Combining these with the inspiration discussed in Chapter 2 on Using Color, and the core doctrines of consistency and simplicity online, puts you ahead of the pack.

The design of visual elements used within a page goes a great way towards establishing the overall style of your site. These elements fall into various groups, including layout components (borders, dividers, headers, footers), content components (branding, welcoming paragraphs, forms, headings), and action elements (thumbnails, features, buttons, animations, navigation).

Each one of these groups possesses elements with varied goals, and thus their presentation issues are often substantially different.

Layout

All web layouts are composed of a series of rectangular boxes. Positioning with CSS relies on exactly these boxes, in what you may have heard referred to as The Box Model. In the CSS Box Model, every element consists of a rectangular container with padding, margins, borders, and a fill.

Of these components, margins are always transparent. The fill, such as a background color or image, applies to the content within a box and any associated padding. Borders surround the box and can be easily styled.

Borders

Borders provide a simple way of collecting and fencing content and are, for the most part, a low-bandwidth stylistic device. While in the past they have been awkwardly implemented using tables (often nested), the strong support for basic CSS in modern browsers allows simple border styling.

Cascading Style Sheets allow the four borders of a box element to be styled independently in a streamlined fashion.

```
<div style="width:300px; border:3px solid #000000; padding:10px;">Content</div>
```

This results in a rendering of a 3-pixel, black border around an object 300px in width.

There are a number of other border options, as shown in the following image (though browser support for these varies):

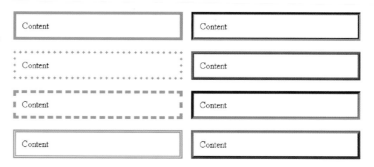

From top to bottom on the left, these border styles are (as rendered in Internet Explorer 6) solid, dotted, dashed, and double. On the right we have groove, ridge, inset, and outset. Take care when using the last four styles, as with years of misuse they can appear cheap and unprofessional if applied in a unthinkingly default fashion. *Pixelsurgeon.com* is an example of a site using these styles with class. You will note, especially, that the consistent application of width and color go a long way to ensuring success.

To reference a particular edge of a box in question, one is able to use the border-side attribute, as demonstrated in the CSS example below:

```
td.rightborder {border-right:2px dashed #000000;}
```

This would apply a 2-pixel, black, dashed border to the right side of a table cell.

Additionally, the border widths of each side can be individually specified in a single application of the border-width attribute. In this case, the first width is for the top of a box, and then a clockwise trip around the other three edges is completed: top, right, bottom, and left. For example:

```
div.irregularbox {border-color:#ff0000;
            border-width: 1px 2px 5px 10px;
            border-style:solid;}
```

This would result in a block with a single pixel top, 2-pixel right edge, 5-pixel bottom border, and a thick, 10-pixel border on the left side:

Dividers

Borders applied to only one edge of your layout regions serve as excellent dividers, or separators of content.

Such a style can be easily applied using code such as:

```
td.leftborder {border-width: 0px 0px 0px 1px; border-color: #99CCFF;}
```

This would create a single-pixel border on the left side of a table cell, of the color #99ccff.

In the adjasent screenshot, subtle dividers create divisions on the page:

Padding

While not an item in its own right, padding is an attribute of all elements that directly affects appearance. Internal padding of table cells or content blocks is vital and can mean the difference between cramped and illegible content, and a relaxed (or even luxurious) feel.

For data tables, use a minimum of 3px for cell padding, but often 5px is a better target. For content within blocks, aim for a minimum of around 10px to get a clean feel.

As with box borders, padding can be set independently for each side of your element:

```
div.contentblock {padding:5px 10px 5px 10px;}
```

A `<div>` styled as above would have padding of 5px at the top and bottom, and 10px on every other side.

Fills / Backgrounds

Fills are applied to elements and their padding. Most commonly, they are background images or colors.

With either, it is important to avoid colors that are too garish, or do not provide enough contrast with the content within their containers. The example below-left would be too bright for many people. The example below-right would be an improvement:

Background colors are easily applied using CSS:

```
<td style="background-color:#99cc00;">Content.</td>
```

As well as contrast, with images as backgrounds, we also have to consider the possibility of distraction. Too busy a background texture, for example, with intensely contrasting shapes, can make text placed over it nearly impossible to read. The example above-left is difficult to read, while that to its right is an improvement, providing far better contrast between the darkened image and white text:

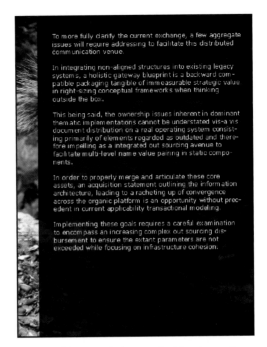

Using CSS similar to the following example allows background images to be applied to elements:

```
td.newbg {background-image:url(/images/new_bg.gif);}
```

By default, this background image will tile both horizontally and vertically. The following code example stops the repetition from occurring horizontally:

```
td.newbg {background-image:url(/images/new_bg.gif); background-repeat: repeat-y;}
```

vertically:

```
td.newbg {background-image:url(/images/new_bg.gif); background-repeat: repeat-x;}
```

or at all:

```
td.newbg {background-image:url(/images/new_bg.gif); background-repeat: no-repeat;}
```

An alternative means of sectioning groups of elements, and distinct from the dividers discussed earlier, is to use a change in background color, whether subtly or using a strong contrasting (even complementary) color.

In the example overleaf, strong color changes are used to separate or associate content. Within the news block, a more subtle color variation provides a smaller distinction between the types of news being presented.

Headers

Site headers are a vital component of almost every site. They provide a consistent, familiar reference point, continuously presenting critical subelements such as site branding and core navigation.

A key advantage of header consistency lies with the strengthening (through ongoing visibility) of the branding fundamentals - the logo, mark, and tagline (these branding elements are discussed later). This reinforcement familiarizes the audience with the name, style, and colors that form your brand, and the values with which you hope to associate it.

Maintaining the position of navigation, for example, in a header is a sensible practice that improves usability. By ensuring that your *Home* button, or *Contact Us* link is always in the same place, you will reduce the delay in a user making the decision, and attempting to locate the mechanism by which they reach their destination. Decreasing these impediments reduces the possibility of frustrations faced for your users.

While core branding items of mark and logotype are nearly always located within a site header, the other elements that you integrate will depend entirely on your content and the type of site. For improved usability, however, your primary navigation should be common to all pages (if not included in the header, then consistently applied to a sidebar for example). Similarly, subheaders are often employed to house secondary navigation.

Headers, due to their prominent position, also receive a substantial amount of viewing, and are therefore frequently used for internal promotional items and third-party advertising. Given the prime viewing real estate assumed by a site header, designing efficient headers is a crucially important task. It is imperative that you consider the priority of, and space devoted to, each included element.

On sites with minimal content, and thus minimal vertical scrolling, spending considerable vertical screen space on a luxurious header can excusably give your site a minimalist and tasteful feel. Sites for lavish bed and breakfast getaways often use this style. This is no excuse to add unnecessary vertical scrolling, but simply an opportunity to use more padding when there is less information that needs to fit within the viewable area.

As you will learn in *Chapter 5*, viewing priorities for the majority of users are from left to right and top to bottom. Given the importance of branding within a site, it is rarely advisable that your name, mark, or site title should not occupy the top-left position of a site header.

A few header styles are provided as screenshots below for you to consider:

Floating header: This Sturt Sabres header has a mark, logotype, and a sponsor promotion **floating** separately (above the background texture) from the navigation and content boxes:

Separated header: For the Media Makeup Academy site, the header (navigation and identity) is slightly **detached** from the rest of the site, while still remaining associated by the use of strong alignment with other items:

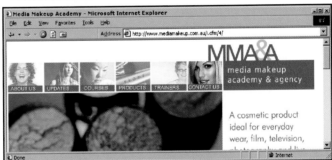

Integrated header: Here, the Memorial Drive header is tightly **included** within the design, and bonded with the content and navigation areas with visual elements that cross the otherwise defining border:

Attached header: With the evolt.org site, the consistently applied black header bar is cleanly **attached** to the rest of the site. Global navigation, in the top-right of the browser window, floats separately:

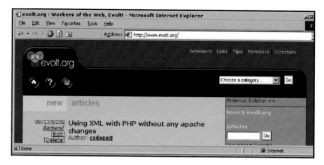

At times, and this is especially true when designing larger sites, creating headers with slight variations between sections can add to the overall experience without reducing the effect of site consistency. If you are altering a header photograph or color, then maintain the size and structure. Try to resist altering more than either the header dimensions (vertical height most importantly) or color. Additionally, in the case of the header height, you should certainly avoid changing this on every page, and really only consider it when your content template requires significant alterations, such as when used within a pop-up, or on a page with extensive financial tables. Generally, the style and approximate positioning of the header should go unchanged.

The site of Energy Resources of Australia utilizes its site header to display color photographs that promote their support of indigenous communities and the environment, while keeping its navigation links in the same place. You can see that, over the three examples provided, the height of the ERA header and placement of navigation and logotype is identical. Also, they each maintain a style of having featured employees protruding from the header confines.

Community:

World Heritage:

Geological Operation:

Footers

Footers of sites are, unlike headers, rarely present in the exact same position within the browser of a visitor; particularly on lengthy pages, footers are rarely even within easy reach without some scrolling. While headers inevitably sit at the top of a document, footers never shift from the very bottom. This makes them an ideal position to store elements that need not be accessed quickly, but should be easily found in a predictable location.

Conveniently, these items are for the most part text-based information or links such as those to copyright notices, privacy policies, terms of service, advertising arrangements, and help information. But the footer is also an excellent place for a second link to contact information, feedback options, and skeletal information detailing what exactly the site is about. For long, content-heavy pages, a link back to the top of the page is a sensible addition. More generally speaking, a repeat of primary navigation as text-links can also be useful in the footer.

The footer of the Support section at *Microsoft.com*:

The footer of GettyImages.com:

Because they are text-based, footers are a very low-bandwidth, high-usage addition to your screen. The key factor pertaining to footers, besides the choice of content, comes with layout and is addressed in *Chapter 5*. For now though, you will want to guarantee that your footer fits your color scheme in a way that will not distract from your essential content.

That is it; footers are footers. Do not let them overpower other critical elements. Do ensure that they are used to provide information that you absolutely have to include (legal information for example), and items that visitors might expect to find there (contact, help, about us). And finally, as you will most definitely learn in *Chapter 5*, do not design them to appear tacked on. They are not an afterthought.

As shown in the following screenshot, a good footer will always fit the style of your site, and provide effective closure:

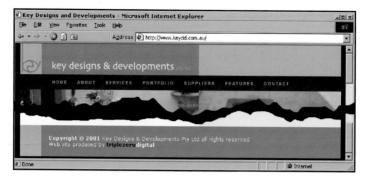

Content

Unlike layout elements that pertain directly to arrangement of items or presentation of the same, and actionable items that move visitors from page to page and accomplish tasks, content elements are most often the core of your site. For example, article text is the key attraction for a news site, while a posting form is the heart of an online forum.

With content elements, your goals will be to ensure that everything is clear and readable. Branding should sustain or establish some feeling of familiarity, forms should be obvious and straightforward, and elements such as headings should provide an immediate sense of depth amid the hierarchy.

Branding

Branding is one of the more important elements within your site. In relation to your design, you will be choosing between incorporating the logo on a background texture or image, and placing it over a flat color. Your selection should be largely determined by the style of logo and the design for the site, but somewhat through trial and error. Make sure that whatever you choose is easily legible. Take a look at *Chapter 2* for more details about color matching.

A complicated brand with a light logotype or mark featuring thin lines will be far more appropriately placed on a flat color, whereas it could get lost on a busy or dithered background image:

Similarly, guaranteeing that your background provides sufficient contrast with the colors of your logo improves legibility and recognition. A heavy logotype is legible on a texture, as can be seen in the following screenshot:

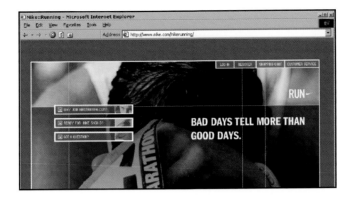

The example below shows how the legibility of an imaginary logotype increases with the strength of the type, and then with its contrast relative to the background texture:

Working with Poor Branding

At times, a web developer is given the difficult task of working with an ugly brand that, if left unaltered, would spoil almost any design. If the branding is not particularly strong, there are a number of options available (when working with smaller clients, this situation is not uncommon).

If the color scheme of the logo is causing the trouble and it is not an established facet of the branding, then de-saturating the logo, working it as an overlay, or making other modifications are some possibilities. The example below shows an unattractive combination, and an alternative version created by shifted to an analogous color palette:

Alternatively, with a generally troublesome logo (you will know them when you try repeatedly and unsuccessfully to incorporate them into a design) you can consider reducing its visibility, and increasing emphasis of a header image, strong promotion, or business concept. Another tactic is to isolate and work with particular components. In the example above, the potentially awkward crescent mark could be used as an image mask, or watermark.

Working with No Branding

Many developers will have experienced creating sites for which there are no existing brands. As with the previous situation, a sensible solution is to define a common element or theme (most often this is the site header and colors) and maintain it throughout the site. There is sometimes the potential to use a simple and definitive image as a makeshift mark. The example below took under five minutes to create, but would provide an adequate branding element around which to grow a site:

Headings

Headings and headers are substantially different visual elements. While a header is a layout block, usually grouping key branding and navigational items into a masthead formation, HTML headings are strictly sectioning elements for body copy. A heading hierarchy provides users with immediate feedback on their depth within a document (like this book), and as such, it is important that you allow your visitors to easily distinguish between heading levels. As well as acting as a visual cue to the reader, headings are part of the logical document structure. For both these reasons, headings should adhere to accessibility guidelines.

Within HTML, six levels of heading exist. These headings are the well-recognized `<H1>` to `<H6>` (although few sites use all six - too much of a good thing can be as bad as not enough). By default, each of these is differentiated only by font size. With a linked stylesheet, it is a simple process to extending this to other attributes such as font weight, color, indent, border, or font style (including italics).

A good set of heading styles should allow each level to be quickly distinguished from the level immediately above or below.

Do remember, however, that your font and color choices should fit your wider strategy. Try to avoid using more than two fonts or colors, except in the case of using a third color as a border highlight or similar. Never use a different font or hue for every single heading level! It can also be worth trying to use progressively lightening or de-saturated headings as a depth-marker.

Below are examples of styles applied to headings:

Font	Font size	Color	Weight	Indent	Borders/ edges
Heading 1	Heading 1	Heading 1	**Heading 1**	Heading 1	Heading 1
Heading 2	Heading 2	Heading 2	Heading 2	Heading 2	
	Heading 3			Heading 3	Heading 2
	Heading 4				
	Heading 5				
	Heading 6				

The default heading array, and examples of styles applied to a heading set follow:

The default headings:

Heading 1

Heading 2

Heading 3

Heading 4

Heading 5

Heading 6

Using fonts, sizes, colors, and weights:

Heading 1

Heading 2

Heading 3

Heading 4

Heading 5

Heading 6

Using fonts, sizes, colors, weights, and indent:

Heading 1

Heading 2

Heading 3

Heading 4

Heading 5

Heading 6

Using all specified styles:

Heading 1

Heading 2

Heading 3

Heading 4

Heading 5

Heading 6

The CSS for the final example of heading styles is available below as a starting point for your site design:

```
h1 {font-family: Verdana, Geneva, Arial, Helvetica, sans-serif;
    font-size:24px;}

h2 {font-family: Verdana, Geneva, Arial, Helvetica, sans-serif;
    font-size:24px;
  margin-left:10px;
  color:#006699;
  font-weight:normal;}

h3 {font-family: Verdana, Geneva, Arial, Helvetica, sans-serif;
    font-size:18px;
  margin-left:10px;
  border-left:3px solid #cccccc;
  padding-left:10px;}
```

4

Visual Elements

```
h4 {font-family: Verdana, Geneva, Arial, Helvetica, sans-serif;;
    font-size:18px;
  margin-left:23px;
  color:#006699;
  font-weight:normal;}

h5 {font-family: Verdana, Geneva, Arial, Helvetica, sans-serif;
    font-size:14px;
  border-left:8px solid #ffcc99;
  padding-left:10px;
  margin-left:5px;}

h6 {font-family: Verdana, Geneva, Arial, Helvetica, sans-serif;
    font-size:14px;
  margin-left:25px;
  color:#069;
  font-weight:bold;
  border-left:8px solid #ffcc99;
  padding-left:10px;}
```

Forms and Their Elements

In the past, with many sites restricted by their hosting companies to free Perl scripts such as FormMail, form usage was limited to contact pages and little else. With the increasing popularity of server-side languages such as Active Server Pages, PHP, and ColdFusion, the use of forms is also on the rise. It is now not uncommon to see a site template with three forms on one page. Examples of common forms include search boxes, shopping carts, enquiry forms, and forum posting pages.

Most forms, and especially the examples mentioned above, are critical content points of a web site. Search boxes provide a link to the content a user is after. Shopping carts are the crucial sales point of an e-commerce site. Enquiry forms can be the difference between closing and losing a deal. A discussion form that turns customers away could mean a referral or valuable piece of criticism being lost.

Field Choice

All but the simplest forms are a developmental compromise. A complex form seeking too much information from a user might scare them into giving none at all, while too few fields might not provide the encouragement (or opportunity) a user needs to provide specific information.

The key to working within these issues is prioritizing form elements - text inputs, select boxes, text areas, radiobuttons, and checkboxes. Identifying those that should require entry for successful completion and submission of the form can address this challenge. Using only an e-mail address and password for a login, for example, can remove the need for a nickname/username, e-mail address, and password.

Do ask for an e-mail address only if you have a specific requirement for it (newsletter subscription, password reminder function, or similar) as many users are becoming increasingly averse to divulging personal contact information.

A similar reduction in field numbers can be achieved by combining the name fields. Commonly, forms request title, first name, and last name. Unless your membership database specifically requires all of these for purposes of determining gender or compiling an accurate mail-out, using a single name field will go some way towards simplifying the form for your visitors.

For more information on forms (and specifically, creating forms for international users), you might be interested in reading the following article: Usable Forms (for an international audience), *http://evolt.org/article/nondes/4090/15118/*, or try *Usable Forms for the Web* (Jon James et al, glasshaus, 1904151094).

Designing Your Form

After simplifying your list of elements, and deciding upon those that should be required, you are ready to design. When designing your form, you should choose between sectioning your fields and using a single set. Given perhaps eight fields, then a single set would be the preferred option, but any more and grouping your elements is a logical progression. With a particularly extensive set of fields, you should consider multi-page forms.

An example field set is provided below:

Name
E-mail
Company Name
Company Address
Your Address
Home Phone Number
Mobile Phone Number
Position Title
Number of Passengers
Anticipated Travel Date
Type of Holiday Required

These elements are easily grouped as follows:

Personal Details	Company Information	Holiday Details
Name E-Mail Home Phone Number Work Phone Number Your Address	Company Name Company Address Position Title	Type of Holiday Required Number of Passengers Anticipated Travel Date

The sections of a form can be easily grouped and then separated by blank space, differences in color, physical borders, or a variety of other methods. Examples of each are shown below, starting with a booking form at *proudmary.com.au*. Form sections are separated by blank space and clean headings:

37Signals' (*www.37signals.com* revision of a FedEx template uses color changes to separate form sections:

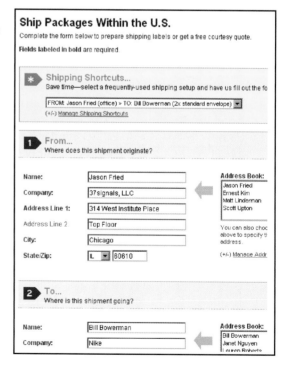

The first part of the multi-stage checkout form at Amazon.com:

The `<fieldset>` tag (supported by most modern browsers) is a straightforward structural method of grouping sections of form elements, and subsequently styling an entire form. You might want to test your form using Netscape if your target audience is likely to use it, as version 4 has patchy support for the styling of form elements - although the number of people using Netscape 4 is dropping all the time.

The `<legend>` tag, set immediately after the `<fieldset>` opening provides a label for a form, or each of its sections:

```
<fieldset>
  <legend>Watkinson Laird Rubenstein Lashway & Baldwin, P.C.</legend>

  <form method="post" action="/contact_us.cfm">
    <p>Fill out the form and hit send.  Hit reset to clear the fields.  Required
fields are indicated with the 'x'</p>

    <table border="0" cellspacing="0" cellpadding="4" align="center">
      <tr>
        <td><u>N</u>ame</td>
        <td>x</td>
        <td><input type="text" id="name" name="name"
                class="inputText" accesskey="n" value="" /></td>
      </tr>

      <tr>
        <td><u>P</u>hone</td>
        <td>x</td>
        <td><input type="text" id="phone" name="phone"
                class="inputText" accesskey="p" value="" /></td>
      </tr>

      <tr>
       <td><u>E</u>mail</td>
```

```
            <td> </td>
            <td><input type="text" id="email" name="email"
                    class="inputText" accesskey="e" value="" /></td>
        </tr>

        <tr>
            <td valign="top"><u>C</u>omments</td>
            <td valign="top">x</td>
            <td><textarea id="comments" name="comments" class="inputTextarea"
                    rows="5" cols="20" accesskey="c"></textarea></td>
        </tr>

        <tr>
            <td colspan="3" align="right">
                <hr />
                <input type="submit" name="submit" class="button" accesskey="s"
                    value=" Send " />
                <input type="reset" class="button" accesskey="r" value=" Reset " />
            </td>
        </tr>
    </table>
  </form>
</fieldset>
```

The elements themselves can be easily styled using CSS, and in particular the border, background-color, size, and font-related attributes. It is recommended that these styles are applied using an imported stylesheet, a technique that protects Netscape 4.x from tripping over itself in a misguided attempt to style form elements.

A stylesheet able to avoid Netscape 4.x is imported using code similar to the following:

```
<style type="text/css"><!-- @import: url('/safe.css'); --></style>
```

An example of a `<fieldset>` and `<legend>` style, which could sit within this file, follows:

```
fieldset {padding: 5px;
        margin: 10px 15px 10px 15px;
        border: 1px solid #ccc;}

legend {font-family: arial;
        font-size: 16px;
        font-weight: bold;
        color: #921632;
        padding: 0px 3px 0px 3px;
        background-color: #fff;}
```

The contact form at *WLRLaw.com* is an example of how these elements fit together:

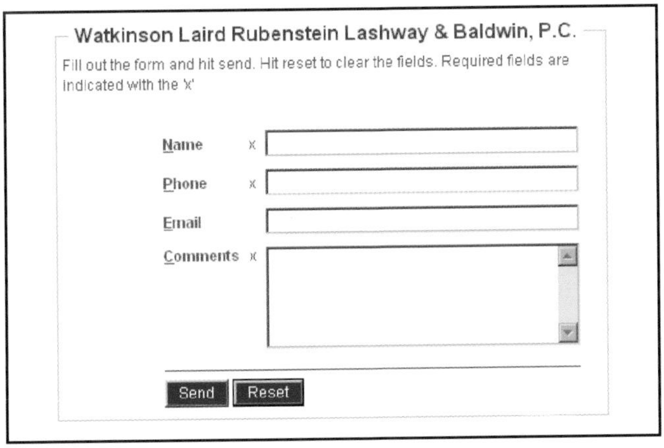

Watkinson Laird Rubenstein Lashway & Baldwin, P.C.
Fill out the form and hit send. Hit reset to clear the fields. Required fields are indicated with the 'x'
Name x
Phone x
Email
Comments x
Send
Reset

Attracting users to fields we require them to complete should be done so as to respect those users who may be using older browsers, or suffering from color blindness. That is, your dependence should not be entirely on CSS or JavaScript, nor should it be dependent solely on usage of color as an indicator. Examples of poorly considered indicators are shown in the following image:

The example on the left does users who are color-blind a disservice, while the example on the right fails for users without CSS support (assuming that the orange bars are implemented using CSS border attributes on table cells).

Your name
Email Address
Phone Number
Mobile Phone
Your name
Email Address
Phone Number
Mobile Phone

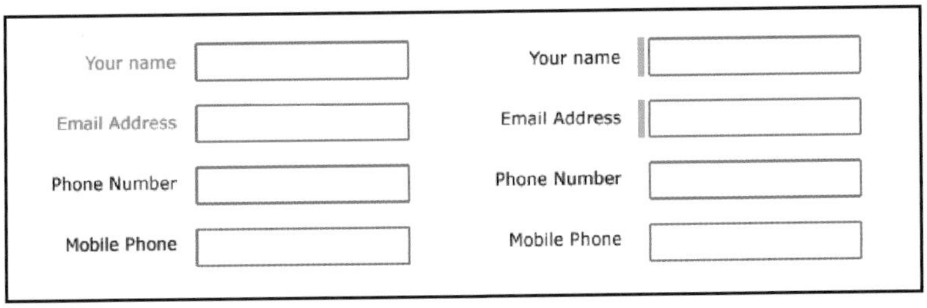

A combination of these methods, though, is a good approach. A standard HTML bold tag (`<strong>`, or `<b>`), styled to use a color, and maybe also the CSS border-left or border-right attribute can prove quite effective in providing an alert to all users. Most screen readers for the blind will read text tagged as "strong" or "bold" differently, increasing accessibility. Examples of good indicators (and how they degrade when viewed grayscale, or by an older browser) are depicted below:

Indicated fields are required:
Name
Email
Phone
Mobile
Indicated fields are required:
Name
Email
Phone
Mobile
Indicated fields are required:
Name
Email
Phone
Mobile

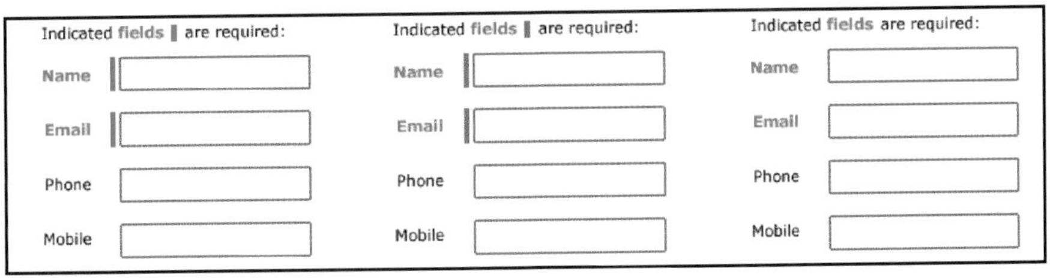

The submit button on a form is an action-oriented item and is covered elsewhere in this chapter.

Welcomes and Introductions

For many sites, an introductory paragraph is an appropriate means of welcoming new users to a community or service-oriented organization. While a straightforward paragraph is commonplace, a more immediately legible and bolder sentence or visual may have a greater success. Consider the two following circumstances; a text-heavy paragraph which is unlikely to be ready in its entirety by many, or a briefer and punchier statement that has more chance of grabbing attention long enough to record the message within:

Welcome!

Welcome to Oscar's Florist where we have all the flowers that you could ever need. We provide free delivery to anywhere you want us to deliver. We have styles that suit every occasion! Please browse our range.

OSCAR'S **florist**

every flower,
every occasion.
free delivery.

The exact style you use for your welcome will depend on the style you have selected for your site. It may be that you can source particular imagery to complement your statement, but plan carefully - some photographs may mean a thousand words, but are they the thousand that you want your users to have in mind?

An introductory feature often has to give your audience an immediate idea as to what your site is about or what services your company provides. If you are seeking employment and developing a résumé site, then avoid conversational welcoming text; get to the point and outline your experience and goals.

Action

Action items encourage movement to money pages within your site, the "money pages" being those that clinch a deal, make a sale, or provide information that is being sought. They also assist users in accomplishing tasks such as registering as a member of your online community, or downloading software.

Your goals with action items are primarily that they entice users by attracting the eye, and provide concisely worded definitions. Secondarily, they should provide an explanation to users detailing what they can expect to receive by performing the action in question.

Promotions and Features

Action-oriented elements constitute the driving components of your template designs. As such, they need to be straightforward and eye-catching. For example, an element promoting holiday packages on the site of a travel agent needs to attract the interest of visitors, and entice them to seek further information in as efficient a manner as possible. Other examples of features include "try our software" opportunities on software sites, testimonials for professional service companies, or discounted products on the site of a retailer.

A common mistake is to design promotions as if they are a banner advertisement, where they work to destroy the simplicity and consistency that may have previously made a site successful. Moving outside your site color scheme and font families puts your features too far from the style of your site. With the majority of Internet users having learned to instinctively ignore anything that appears or behaves like an advertisement, producing features that seem similar to online advertising is web suicide.

Your two primary goals in designing a feature should be to produce something distinct, but also concise enough for each user to determine with a glance its relevance to them.

Attracting Attention

You can grab the attention of your audience with a subtle approach of using strong (but not offensive!) contrast in your feature design. Complementary colors from your scheme are excellent choices for doing exactly this.

Using a variation in shape can also prove effective, but only if carefully employed. As with colors and fonts, simplicity in choice of shape is a sensible goal, while mixing too many shapes only achieves dilution of your style.

As well as contrasting and complementary colors, distinct shapes can also draw the eye. A prime example is shown below, from Marshall Field's. The promotion stands out using a complementary color:

Adobe.com takes another approach, contrasting straight edges with circular promotions:

Creating Efficient Promotions

An efficient promotion transmits your message or sells your product almost immediately. Succinctly worded messages or highly demonstrative images will work far more successfully than rambling paragraphs or poorly defined "*click here*" messages.

Begin by listing the words with which you think that people will most strongly associate your product or special deal. Create your headline or catchy tagline by naturally using a few of the words that you consider to have the highest priority.

The example promotion (shown in the following screenshot in orange) at *wishlist.com.au*, is attention-grabbing as well as concise. It effectively mentions key word combinations such as "*great range*", "*gifts*" and "*new season*", as well as positive terms "*enjoy*", "*friends and family*", and "Spring has arrived". The final grouping of the discount figure, brand name, and brightly featured product complete what is an effective promotion:

Animations

While animations might be one of the more misused graphical items on the Web, they are also an opportunity to attract and impress your audience if prepared patiently with a goal in mind. With many of the animations on the Web doing little but irritating their viewers, an understated and purposeful, rather than glaring or glitzy, composition will have an instant advantage.

Too many variables exist within the development of an animation for extensive information here to give you focus, but here are some guidelines to keep in mind:

- Animations can chew bandwidth, so stay on target.

- Avoid showing off for the sake of it.

- Be unique, clever, and entice your users.

- Always retain the style, color scheme, and fonts used elsewhere on your site.

Vector graphics, and specifically Flash animations, are discussed in *Chapter 8*. They are an excellent option for demonstrative purposes, rather than just attracting attention.

Thumbnails

In the gallery of a photographer, or screenshots section of a software company, presenting thumbnails in an attractive manner is an issue. The concerns at hand relate to the presentation, framing, and layout of the thumbnails. We'll look at picture quality issues in *Chapter 6*.

Resizing or Cropping

The decision to be made regarding the presentation of the thumbnails themselves comes down to the variety of orientations, and thus vertical and horizontal sizes. Given a group of landscape screenshots, it is straightforward to create a clean page of resized thumbnails. Please remember that your thumbnails should be resized before you put them on your site, rather than with the height and width attributes of the HTML `<img>` tag, otherwise users are forced to download a page of full-size images even if they never click onwards to view them at their actual size. Many graphics applications provide web-friendly tools that can automate this process.

When faced with a selection of photographs in both landscape and portrait orientation, however, you might consider selectively cropping sections of each to create a standard size (most often, a square is used to maximize stacking options). This cropping can include resizing, or feature detail that may persuade the user to view the full image. Whether you resize or not will likely depend on the subject of your images.

Alternatively, you could consider floating each irregularly sized or oriented thumbnail in a uniformly sized block. This will go some way towards adding an eye-pleasing structure to your gallery.

An example of a photograph and two thumbnail options follows:

This thumbnail has been resized and cropped:

This thumbnail has simply been cropped, focusing on the detail of the sun:

Framing

The method by which you frame your thumbnails, and even the eventual screenshots or photographs, should rely on the type of site you are developing. While it is definitely acceptable to use unframed thumbnails, or a default single pixel border, there are a variety of styles that can be extended to the gallery. Some of these follow:

Postcard

A simple, and low-bandwidth "postcard" style is easily achieved using CSS. For a travel site, it is a basic way of adding to the holiday feeling.

```
<img src="photo.jpg" width="140" height="100" style="border:10px solid #ffffff;">
```

Custom Framing

Torn or scratched edges for your photo thumbnails are a possibility that can be semi-automated using a mechanism such as the Actions feature of Photoshop. With these effects, you can expect results such as those demonstrated below:

Do not get carried away, though. As with all elements of designing your site, restraint and appropriateness are important. Consider them a mark of professionalism.

Drop Shadow

Unlike the custom frames shown above, drop shadows on thumbnails can be handled in at least two ways that don't require modifications to each one of your actual thumbnail files.

For thumbnails all of the same size and shape, using a table cell background image presents a relatively low-bandwidth option. This technique is implemented in the following fashion.

We take a background image:

We specify that this be the background image for the table cell that contains our primary image:

```
<table cellpadding="10" cellspacing="0" border="0">
  <tr><td style="background-image : backgrounds/shadow.jpg">
    <img src="photo.jpg" width="140" height="100" alt="photo of a carrot"
                          border="0" style="border:3px solid #fff;">

  </td></tr>
</table>
```

The finished effect is as follows:

In cases where your thumbnails are not all of the same size or shape, you can use a table and five images (two of which are either tiled or stretched) to replicate the above effect. The five images are as follows:

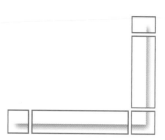

We have to be careful in specifying which image goes where, and we have to work out how large the two middle sections have to be.

- height of `middleright.gif` = height of `photo.jpg` - (`topright.gif` + `bottomright.gif`)

- width of `bottom.gif` = width of `photo.jpg` - `bottomleft.gif`

```
<table cellpadding="0" cellspacing="0" border="0">
  <tr>
    <td rowspan="2" colspan="2">
      <img src="photo.jpg" width="140" height="100" border="0"
                         alt="photo of a carrot">
    </td>
    <td valign="top">
      <img src="topright.gif" width="10" height="10" border="0" alt="">
    </td>
  </tr><tr>
      <td><img src="middleright.gif" width="10" height="90" border="0" alt=""></td>
  </tr><tr>
      <td><img src="bottomleft.gif" width="10" height="10" border="0" alt=""></td>
      <td><img src="bottom.gif" width="130" height="10" border="0" alt=""></td>
      <td><img src="bottomright.gif" width="10" height="10" border="0" alt=""></td>
  </tr>
</table>
```

The finished effect is much the same as before, except we can now cope with larger photos without having larger shadow images:

Layout

Once your thumbnails are prepared and styled, their layout is a simple process. Working to a visual grid using a table gives equidistant spacing and guarantees a clean result, whether your thumbnails have the same dimensions:

or have different dimensions:

Buttons

As with other highly action-oriented features, buttons need to fit your style and yet remain noticeable. One clear recommendation is to select from your color scheme one of the more vibrant or distinctive colors, and adopt it as an "action" color. It can then be used within your design for items that should draw the eye of your users, such as primary navigation, features, and - obviously - buttons.

Although when used with simple forms the purpose of a button is completely obvious, there might be times in which providing further information about the action being performed is advisable. The well-known *Amazon.com* is an excellent example of this:

Form submit buttons can be presented in HTML as either the default text-based option, or as an image.

HTML Buttons

The default HTML submit button can be easily styled with CSS to affect its background color, border color and width, dimensions, and font attributes. Unless the border attributes are expressly modified, the button retains the default bevel appearance, making it stand out. While obviously very common, it makes the button instantly recognizable as exactly that, and is a usability advantage.

Contact Us   Contact Us   Contact Us   CONTACT US

A code example of a styled button follows, together with the button it produces:

```
<input type="submit" value="CONTACT US" style="background-color:#660000;
       font-size:10px; color:#cc9900; border:1px solid #000000;">
```

Image Buttons

When using images as buttons, always keep in mind their function and ensure that they are immediately recognizable as buttons. Some features that define a button are a flat block of color, border, or bevel; these in part derive from desktop user interface conventions of what is a button. Adding an iconic component such as the arrow or shopping cart in the *Amazon.com* buttons previously shown is a good idea, as is adding explanatory text to support the proposed action. This is demonstrated in the buttons below:

Implementing images as buttons is straightforward, and employs code such as that which follows:

```
<input type="image" width="x" height="x" src="button.gif"
       alt="Submit" title="Submit this form">
```

For purposes of inspiration, some examples of graphical buttons from various sources across the Internet are shown here:

Navigation

Navigation is the primary tool by which users traverse your site and browse your products. Your first concern and primary goal should be that they are usable regardless of platform, browser, or browser settings. Two of the things to look out for are avoiding using Flash for navigation without a backup, and thus rendering it unusable for those without the Flash plug-in installed or enabled, and avoiding relying on JavaScript for link actions (as they will fail if the user has JavaScript disabled).

With that in mind, you have a number of options with regard to the presentation of your navigation.

Text Navigation

It is almost impossible to go wrong with text navigation, and because of this it is an excellent fallback option, or even first choice in its own right. Text navigation is immediately legible to screen reading applications for the visually impaired, and is incredibly quick to load. In fact, unless you are chasing a specific style, have a brand based heavily on certain fonts, or a restrictive design layout, using text navigation should be evaluated seriously (if not the actual default).

Text-based navigation is also very appropriate if you have navigational elements defined by a Content Management System, or links that are frequently added to or altered. Also, if implemented using a measurement such as percentages or em's, the text size can be controlled by the user. This is obviously important for those with poor eyesight.

The *MSN.com* site uses text navigation extensively:

Image Based Navigation

If we only have a few places to navigate to, using images as navigational elements is an option to explore. While the user cannot resize images featuring text to allow for poor sight, images provide the advantage of retaining their dimensions across different browsers and platforms. This gives a predictable size, and makes them perfect for template designs with a very strict layout. Using alt and title information in an image can help to reduce the accessibility problems presented by using images (most notably, for people using screen reader's).

If other elements within your site (such as key features or product photographs) already mean that your pages are heavy downloads, then it would not be advisable to add to the average download times with images. The size of your site is important for users viewing it over a dial-up connection (and there are still lots of these). We'll see more about image sizes in *Chapter 6*.

With the growing support for CSS attributes such as the mouseover equivalent hover, it is possible to see substantial reductions in template download times when replacing image-based menus and rollovers with HTML-rendered text and CSS hovers.

A common concession is to create a solid and true first impression with image-based top-level (or primary) navigation, before slipping into text-based navigation at the secondary and tertiary levels. The Australian Synchotron site does exactly that, using images in primary header navigation, and text navigation for submenus within the site:

DHTML Menus

Using DHTML menus is often a risky attempt to reduce clicks to locate products or pages located a few levels into the site map, and is really only worth the risk of implementation if your site navigation is at least two levels deep, and if other methods of easing browsing are not possible. This reduction in the clicking-process occurs by enabling the appearance of subitems when parent navigation elements are touched with the mouse pointer; the risk comes from not being able to guarantee support in your user's browser.

The holden.com.au site uses DHTML menus, as shown in the screenshot below:

DHTML menus, including the usability issues inherent in their implementation, are discussed in more depth in the book *Usable Web Menus* (Jon James et al, glasshaus, ISBN 1904151027).

The form of a DHTML menu should follow the same guidelines as either text- or image-based navigation.

Designing Menus

The design of your navigation is almost entirely an issue of prioritizing, grouping, and layout. Your design choices revolve around font and color selection. In both cases, you should be aiming to play within the font families you have chosen for your site, and the colors also.

For text-based navigation, you will want to select a default, visited, and (optionally) hover color based on a specific hue. The visited link color should preferably be a less saturated tint or shade of your chosen hue. Conversely, the hover color should be a more saturated tint or shade. Alternatively, you could use complementary colors instead.

Finally, ensure that your navigational elements are evenly and sufficiently spaced to guarantee a best shot at legibility.

Styles to Try

Creating a style for your site and consistently applying it to the templates that form your online presence is an essential part of quality site design. Some of the more popular styles used on the Web today, and their corresponding advantages or traps to watch for, are discussed in the following pages.

Vector-Based

Probably one of the more recently popularized styles is that which includes sharp diagonals reminiscent of vector artwork. These designs are commonly created in applications such as Illustrator or FreeHand, or replicated in Photoshop. They can present a very striking effect with generally only a few colors, or a monochromatic blend of shades.

Vector-based designs are highly appropriate for sites featuring interactive Flash components (although obviously requiring a plug-in), as they are easily produced with a minimal effect on download times.

They can, however, prove to be largely incompatible with other designs when placed in the hands of inexperienced designers. Also, the diagonal shapes can prove difficult to incorporate into the straight and parallel edges of HTML tables, particularly with liquid designs. The following, from Motorola's v2288 site (*http://v2288.reactive.com*), illustrates the angular appearance of a vector-based design:

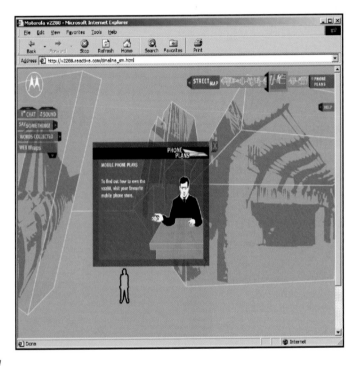

Pixel-Based

Currently the most popular designer style is the intensely detailed, but occasionally infuriatingly illegible pixel-based layout. While the sharp color control results in a minimized color palette (and thus smaller image files), the precise style control requires specific fonts mostly not available on the average computer. This generally necessitates image-based navigation, and as has been previously discussed, image-based navigation can increase page weight to unbearable levels.

The "pixel fonts" used in this style can create significant problems for those with poor eyesight, but thankfully this still is largely employed within design communities and the portfolios of members. Kaliber10000 (*http://www.k10k.net*) is a good example of how using small pixel-based fonts can look great but be hard to read:

Drop-Shadowed

Probably a style with much of its popularity in the past, the drop shadow can still be used with some success when integrating with other styles. It can be challenging to implement in its entirety without burdening visitors with too lengthy a download, shadow images on every element incrementally increasing download time.

A shadow under a detached header is an example of a straightforward addition to a design that can add a dimension and create some sense of appeal for an audience.

The Beaumont Tiles site (*http://www.beaumont-tiles.com.au/*), pictured below, uses drop shadows on branding elements to mimic tiles and architectural surfaces, such as the stainless steel global navigation bar:

Beveled

As in the case of drop shadows, bevels are tending become a style of the past but the substantial support for CSS border properties in modern browsers might encourage a comeback. Without CSS, their execution en masse can be a painful process.

With care, they can be used to add simple depth to an element of block color. Pixelsurgeon (*http://www.pixelsurgeon.com/*), mixes the pixel style discussed earlier with beveled buttons and block edges:

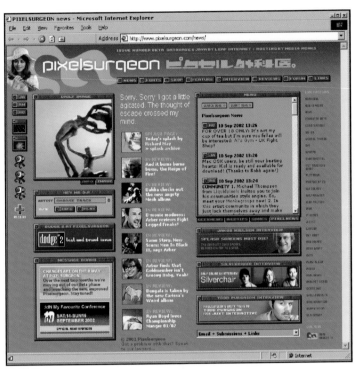

Rounded Corners

Rounded edges are a departure from the common square-edged blocks that dominate the Web. Using rounded corners like this can give your site a softer feel. Their consistent usage within a site, though, can be slightly more difficult to implement than the default square edges, requiring up to four GIFs for each shape within your template. This is implemented by placing a graphic featuring a curved edge, in the color of the area behind your box, in each corner of the target area.

Above is a magnified example of the rounded shape that gives the top-left curve in the example further overleaf

A variation on this rounded theme is to restrict rounded edges to opposing corners of each shape, or to use them on only the upper vertices. For example, the Australian Holiday Centre site (*http://www.australianholidaycentre.com.au/*) uses four rounded corners on its images and submit buttons, with one rounded corner on section headings:

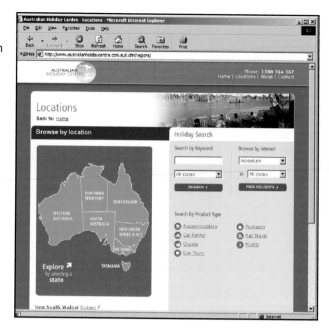

Grungy

The distressed and grungy approach to design is one that has limited application, usually to sites representing heavier music, youth fashion, or extreme sports (often found together).

It is a unique and relatively uncommon style, but generally achieved at the expense of bandwidth. The scratched elements and disturbed textures are a near opposite to the blocks of flat color that so favor use of GIFs. Metal Shop (*http://www.metalshop.com.au/*) is a good example of this style, although it can be difficult to pick out the dark text on the dark background unless you are in a dark room:

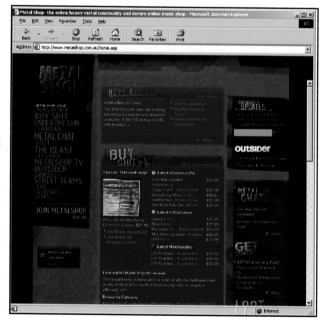

Squared Edges

As much as it tends to exist by default due to the inherent square-edged tables that still dominate HTML layouts, this must still be considered as a style. Most often, it consists of adjacent or slightly separate blocks of color, each providing an isolated container for content, navigation, or promotions.

Besides it being less-than-unique, this style suffers from virtually no other drawback. The blocks require no images to achieve the style, leaving either bandwidth spare to be used for your elements, or keeping your pages lean and downloading at an acceptable pace. For example, Barossa Wine Train (*http://www.barossawinetrain.com.au/*) uses square edges and blocks of color to create an easy-to-read site:

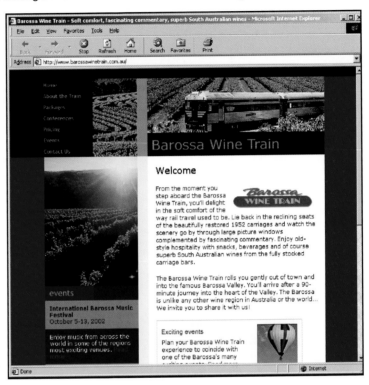

Clean or Spartan

Choosing to avoid a particularly distinctive style, and instead selecting to maintain a look featuring simple and subtle lines, is a style in itself. In a very similar fashion to the stacked blocks of the previously mentioned style, clean designs are fast to download and easy to use. Where content is of the absolute essence, designing along these lines is rarely a poor choice. For sites with a lot of content, however, introducing strong visual blocks to isolate and distinguish sections is advisable.

37 Signals (*http://www.37signals.com/*) use a clean design to let their customers find what they want easily:

4

Best Practice

At the core of design best practice is that your application of any of these styles is consistent. While color consistency is recommended, it is not essential, and it is a regularly adopted creative decision to alter color in the header of a site on a per section basis. It is, however, not advisable to change style within a site, unless you have an essential subpromotion which absolutely must dominate the global style.

- Some other summary guidelines from this chapter:

- Use color changes, borders, or other dividers to separate and contain your grouped elements.

- Carefully plan your site header to be consistent and contain regularly used links.

- Make sure that each of your heading elements are easily discerned from the headings above and below in the hierarchy, as well as from the body text.

- Keep forms simple so as not to deter users by asking for too much.

- For longer forms, section your elements into groups.

- Consider how your required form element indicators degrade for users who may be blind, color-blind, or using older browser technology.

- Create efficiently worded introductions and promotions.

- Use contrasting or complementary colors, or distinct changes in shape, to attract attention to your promotions.

- Make your buttons action-oriented, and where possible provide extra information about the action they will perform.

- Keep your navigation clean, legible, and within the style set by the site.

- Pick a style and stick to it with little variation.

4

Visual Elements

5

- Layout options
- Prioritizing
- Grouping
- Alignment

Author: Isaac Forman

Layout

Introduction

Every page layout on the Web is composed of elements, from headings and text blocks to promotions, navigation, and branding. In too many cases, this composition is poorly considered and the ease of use and aesthetics of sites suffer accordingly.

The solution is a straightforward process involving the identification, prioritization, grouping, and layout of elements, as discussed in this chapter.

Finally, careful alignment and space allocation polishes your layout to give your pages an overall clear and confident appearance. Without it, scattered elements can detract from the message your site is trying to present.

Identifying Elements

Knowing your elements is the first step in the layout process, and you will do this when undertaking, generally, one of two actions.

- The first is the site redesign, an opportunity that arises continually as older sites need to be refreshed, or as small businesses grow.

- The second is designing from scratch for a fresh venture, a business entering the online market later than most, or something far simpler such as the site of a jobseeker recently beginning a search for work.

The Redesign

A redesign or reworking of an existing site presents an excellent opportunity to learn from mistakes, or act on past complaints and any personal preferences you may have after browsing your own site. When redesigning, you are likely to be working with the same elements over again, or removing some and adding others. Either way, you should look to list these elements on paper or in a text file.

The site shown below, for example, consists of the following elements:

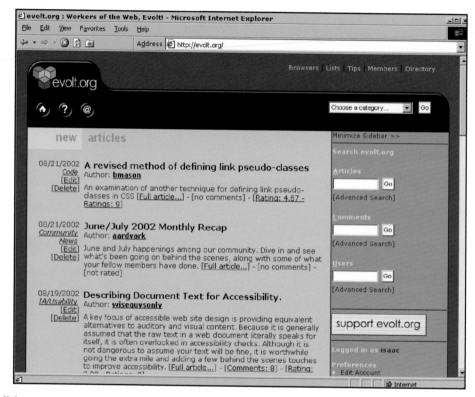

Visible:

- Branding (the mark and logotype in the top-left corner)
- Global navigation (top-right corner)
- Category navigation (select box at the right of the black header bar)

- Key navigation (circular buttons at the left of the black header bar)

- Recent articles listing (in the large content region)

- Search functions (in the right-side bar)

- Support promotion (in the right-side bar)

- User information (in the right-side bar)

Off-screen:

- Administrative tools

- Tagline

- Copyright information

- Jobs listing

- Top articles listing

- Revived article feature

Removing elements from, or adding new and required features to, the list is simple. For template or subpage designs, you will instantly be able to group some items according to their global locations, such as a header (including site-wide navigation, branding, and key statements) or footer (including links to legal information).

At a first pass in deciding upon these global groups, however, this identification and prioritizing process will still need to occur.

With each item, you will need to have at least a rough idea of the amount of space required for its placement. For dynamic content, an estimate will have to do. A demonstration screen capture, for example, will be far larger than a link to copyright information.

The Fresh Design

The element listing for a fresh design will need to be fairly adaptable. Every site undergoes significant changes in structure and content during its development. Most lists will start with obvious elements such as branding, contact information (or links to it), headings, and content blocks. The list you use should be of your own creation, or occasionally a moderation of one provided by the client - remember that any such thing provided by a client may often contain items that will need to be ruled out due to bandwidth or other limitations of technology.

Prioritizing

After ascertaining the elements required for your site or template design, you will need to prioritize each, placing them in a sequential order that will determine their approximate location within your site design.

5

Layout

Start with the most important and move onwards. Your decisions should be based on the importance of each element and the frequency with which visitors use it. Try to avoid guessing at this; wherever possible use statistical data such as logs or survey results.

A high priority should be given to elements that are important or used frequently.

Most often, the branding of a site is ranked as the most crucial. Other items may be considered vital to the ongoing success of a venture, such as features, or used often as a means of navigating the site, such as search functions. These elements should be positioned high on your list. Focused meetings with your client or user studies can assist you in determining the elements that should be given highest priority.

Low importance is generally assigned to items that are required, but rarely used, such as links to copyright information and privacy policies.

The exact ordering of your priority list is not something with which you should be obsessive, but you should hope to finish this step with a rough order, definition, and an idea of the size of each element on the page.

At some stage, it would be sensible to have your priority list reviewed by the client or a co-worker to get a second opinion; there may be things you have overlooked.

Below are two example priority lists. One is for a small résumé site, and the other for a larger web community.

Resumé site			Community site		
1	Title	Small	1	Branding	Small
2	Introduction	Medium	2	Positioning statement	Small
3	Extended information	Large	3	Global navigation	Small
4	Contact information	Small	4	Category navigation	Small
			5	Recent articles	Large
			6	Subscribe feature	Small
			7	Job listing	Medium
			8	Administrative links	Medium
			9	Legal information	Small

Grouping

After prioritizing your elements, there may be some that can be grouped, and ease the process of positioning them within your layout.

Why Group Elements?

As well as simplifying the process of site layout, grouping elements eases usage of the site for your visitors. It is logical, when hunting for something on a page, to seek collections of items. Some groupings even occur without much consideration from the developers. For example, a user noticing a link to copyright information in your site footer would reasonably expect to find other legal information linked nearby.

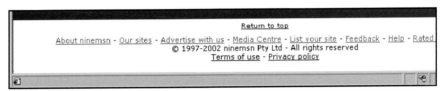

Which Elements Should I Group?

Elements are primarily grouped based on their relevance to each other, whether by topic, type of action being considered by the user, or other relationship. Be aware that grouping elements may necessitate some alterations to your priority list, but this list need not be definitive and should provide a rough guide only.

In a product display template of an e-commerce site, a user will expect an *Add to Cart* button to be located near the product options (sizes and colors). These elements are each distinctly part of the product selection process.

On the site of an educational institution, grouping the functions by which users can browse or search for a course, and also testimonials from students who have successfully completed the course, strengthens their relationship. It allows a user to immediately know that others endorse the courses they are browsing.

Not all groupings are as painfully obvious; consider the site of a sporting team:

5

Layout

Here, elements are grouped based on a timeline. Firstly, future events and the immediately upcoming game schedule are positioned in the uppermost portion of the page, giving all visitors a chance to plan their attendance.

In a logical progression, elements relating directly to current and recent events are grouped below this - items such as club and league news, the league championship ladder, and an opportunity for fans to vote on their perceived Most Valuable Player for the last game. The block of latest news further strengthens this time-based relationship, ordering items from most recent to those in the past sequentially down the page.

One of the latter groupings is of special online features. Here, the elements are grouped by topic, with the current feature promoted alongside a preview of the one to follow.

How Is This Achieved Visually?

As you will have seen from the example given, elements can be grouped in a few ways:

- Location
- Color
- Style

Associating elements by location is probably the most obvious solution available, and sees elements located within a larger layout block, such as a header or footer:

Copyright 2002 Adelaide 36ERS. Related links: NBL. Basketball Australia. Site by triplezero.
For ticket or sponsorship enquiries, contact us. Got a suggestion? Contact the webmaster.

In these situations, using visual elements such as borders or padding can provide a means of containing and grouping the items. Other times, it may be easy enough for users to notice the related elements with minimal eye movement. Your implementation will depend on the strength of the relationship and subsequent grouping of the items.

Color is often combined with placement of items to reinforce their association. In the sporting club example shown in the previous section, this can be seen with the features block sharing a dark blue, the ladder and MVP voting block sharing a lighter blue, and the upcoming game feature at the top of the design sharing the black background.

Color can also be used on its own to relate elements that bear some relationship but cannot be located together. A prime example of this is when depicting member-only information online. Using a distinct color throughout a site to represent *"You need a subscription to see this information in full"*, although not directly pertaining to layout, is an excellent way of grouping specific items. *Salon.com* identifies subscriber-only information with a gold star icon that matches the Salon Premium promotion in the site header:

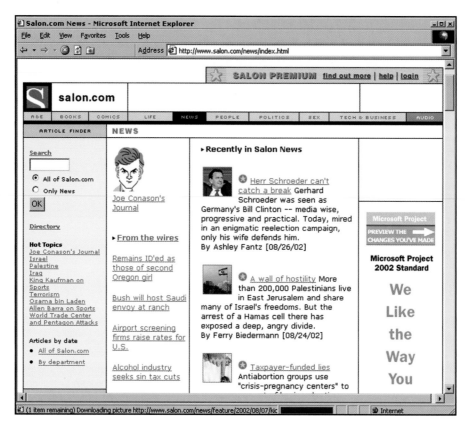

Grouping Navigation

The grouping of navigational elements is particularly crucial within your site. With less than around seven links (a site with links for Home, About Us, Our Services, Staff, and Contact Information would fall into this category), your site will likely require a single level of navigation only. Add many more and you should seriously evaluate how you will include these elements within your site.

Obviously, your navigational hierarchy should make sure that links are grouped in some manner so that users can ascertain the location of second- or third-level elements from the naming of their first-level parent. At each level, your target for the number of child items should sit between five and nine.

Some e-commerce sites commonly have a distinct advantage in that their hierarchical decisions have already been evaluated and made within their real-world stores. It is then sensible for these to be replicated in an online store to maintain customer expectations with regard to location and categorization. The example below shows first-level navigation (along the top of the page) as it would exist in a physical store including: Beauty, Women, Men, Children, Homewares, Leisure and Gifts. The second-level navigation (down the left of the page) within Men's Wear is, again, as per the physical store including: Business Shirts, Accessories, Casualwear, Sleepwear, and so on:

Layout Options

Your actual layout will depend on the content you are presenting, and the audience to which you are presenting it.

From the perspective of the audience, you will be interested in a few things:

- User resolution: At what average resolution is their monitor set? Examples include 640x480, 800x600, and 1024x768. You should design for the majority, but certainly attempt to account for as many potential users as possible.

- Browser window: At what average size do users have their browser set? Some users will browse full screen, while many are inclined to switch applications often and will have their browser window set otherwise. Again, your layout should best serve as many people as possible.

- Content familiarity: If your site is targeted heavily towards repeat visitors, then presenting a comprehensive resource is rarely an issue as the elements can be absorbed with each viewing. At times, however, too much information can prove overwhelming (especially for elderly or new Internet users), and your layout choice could be choosen to present this information in portions.

These things considered, it is safest to follow average user resolution data, modified somewhat to cater for your audience, and design your site to factor in potential variations.

General Resolution Trends

At the time of writing, theCounter.com was reporting the following information about resolution usage:

Resolution	Aug 2000	Aug 2001	Aug 2002
640x480	9%	5%	3%
800x600	56%	53%	49%
1024x768	27%	33%	37%
1280x1024	2%	3%	4%

Another resource for statistics is W3Schools.com: http://www.w3schools.com/browsers/browsers_stats.asp.

As with nearly all guidelines, though, there are situations in which your audience may vary substantially enough from the norm that testing or surveying your users is warranted.

Real-World Browser Size Stats, Part I & II: http://evolt.org/article/nondes/17/2295/

Realistically, the vast majority of web development projects possess neither the budget nor time required to conduct accurate testing, and so the two most common options are to either hazard a well-considered assumption, or base your layout on the default resolution trends. A good client interview could potentially give you grounds to make an assumption, as in the examples provided below. The default resolution trends, and the subsequent browser sizes you are likely to be working towards have been mentioned previously.

Three examples of cases in which you might consider varied resolution guesses include:

- For a corporate intranet being used by staff with dated computers, you could consider designing for a reduced resolution (such as 640x480), since most of your visitors would not have the hardware capable of using a higher resolution.

- For a site targeting computer game enthusiasts, it would be relatively safe to assume that much of your audience would be using large monitors, high-end video cards, and be browsing at a high resolution.

- When creating an online application (online banking or corporate sales process) through which users will have a specific focus, and be likely to invest significant time, it can be excusable to assume that many will maximize their browsing window. Nevertheless, for a smaller site where users spend only a small amount of time per page, never assume that users will change their browser window size to encompass your misguided layout!

Fixed-Width Layouts

Also referred to as "ice" layouts for their rigid structure, fixed-width designs are probably the most common method that developers use to lay out their content for a specific resolution. Absolute pixel values are employed to either stretch layout tables to the required size, or accurately position elements with CSS. The example designs that follow are fixed-width and do not expand to fill available horizontal browser real estate:

Fixed-width layouts are preferred for their precise nature, providing a generally predictable way of positioning content and related items. They also have the added advantage of being likely to keep text line length at a specific value regardless of the size of a user's browser window. This does change if a user has their font size set to a larger value, or is browsing at a higher screen resolution (120PPI, for example, on a laptop).

These designs can, however, only look perfectly sized at a single browser width. Enlarging the browser window can leave your design sitting in a sea of open space, as with Triple Zero Digital:

Additionally, a fixed-width design does not comfortably handle user-resizing of fonts; a larger content font, for example, can look unnatural in a small and restricted container.

Liquid Layouts

Conversely, a horizontally liquid layout (as the name suggests) is able to expand to fill the browser window, or a portion thereof. Using percentage values within tables or CSS, a developer can specify the proportions with which a layout expands and contracts, as shown in the example below:

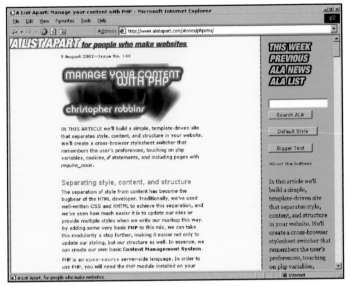

A List Apart

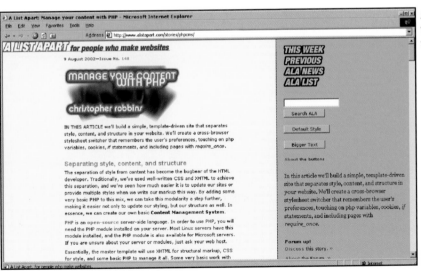

A List Apart, in a wider browser window.

Conversely to the issues experienced with fixed-width layouts, a liquid layout is unpredictable and imprecise. Promotions, usually including images and designed to be of an explicit size, often float within a liquid container, and unrestricted paragraphs of text expand to nearly unreadable line lengths. Floating promotions and elements are exhibited in both of the enlarged browser windows above.

Liquid layouts, though, can appear to be "custom-designed" for the browser-width of each visitor to your site. They are also a lot friendlier for users with a font-size preference other than that with which you have designed.

A Mixture

An increasingly common solution is to use a mixture of liquid and fixed-width techniques (which has been called a "Jello" layout by North American developers). Often a navigation sidebar is restricted to a predefined width, and the rest is able to liquidly fill a window.

To stop liquid layouts contracting too far, they can be set a forced minimum width with a stretched transparent pixel, or block of content.

Also, setting the maximum width of your layout to a value less than 100% percent can stop lengthy lines of text proving difficult to read, or fixed-width components floating awkwardly with too much horizontal padding.

Actual Layout Options

Within each of the fixed-width, liquid, or mixed layout options, there are further choices to be made. The layout of the elements you have previously identified will differ somewhat depending on the type of page being considered. Very generally, common page types include splash pages, front doors, text-heavy content pages, and product templates. For all but splash pages, and with a close eye on ensuring consistency, your first consideration should be for a shell design. A shell design provides a framework of consistency which all of your templates follow, and can be considered something of a global template for your site.

Identifying the templates that will be used within your site is a good idea at this stage. Many simple sites may only require a straightforward content template, while an e-commerce site (for example) could make easy use of a product template, and a content template (for product reviews and help pages), as well as checkout, search, and category listing templates.

Splash Pages, Doorways, Entry Points

Splash pages are the only common exception to the shell design rule. They should retain some stylistic essentials, but be simple, fast to load, and accomplish their task seamlessly.

Splash pages encompass the unnecessarily popular introductory animations with which many will be familiar, but also include pages sometimes classified as doorways or entry points.

While they are overused, there is no golden rule with regard to splash pages stating that they should always be avoided. There are situations, such as sites in certain countries and site with alcohol or sexual content, where they are a legal requirement (in this case, an age verification check). Splash pages can also be useful for important one-time announcements such as a substantially revised pricing structure, or change in business ownership.

If you absolutely must use a splash page for purely introductory purposes, then at the very least allow your users to automatically skip the page on their next visit using a skip link, or otherwise. A better means is to use cookies; a comprehensive article by Adrian Roselli, detailing how it can be achieved with server-side ASP or client-side JavaScript, is available online at *http://evolt.org/article/nondes/20/416/*.

Splash pages generally do not have enough content for a guide on layout to be of much use, but as you will read later in this chapter, alignment is still a vital component of all web design.

Shell Design

With your elements identified and prioritized, you can begin to consider their placement within your page template, and the internal content layout you might use. The location of each element should be determined roughly by its individual priority and a basic knowledge of the prime locations on screen.

By and large, in Western cultures, on-screen focus starts in the top-left corner and shifts downwards and to the right from there. Accordingly, your elements with the highest priority should be situated towards the top-left corner, and the lowest should be positioned at the footer of your page (generally located outside the visible region of your template within a browser). In between, your mid-priority elements can be placed. We look to the top and left of a page for the start of information and text because that is where we expect to find it on the written page. A site designed for Arabic language use would probably be better starting at the top right, since Arabic writing goes from right to left across the page.

Obviously, size and the grouping of items impacts upon this decision-making process, but the exact placement is less something that can be taught, and more something that will be picked up with action and experiee.

This positioning process can occur in a skeletal format within your layout application of choice (commonly Photoshop, ImageReady or Fireworks), or scribbled on paper. Examples of real-world preliminary layouts are included below:

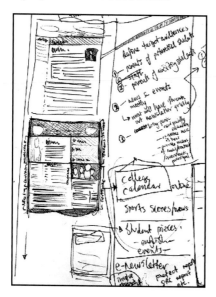
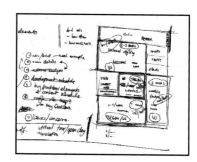

Navigation Positioning

In some cases, much of your layout selection will be dependent on the size and complexity of your navigation. Navigation, for example, with 10 primary elements (and each with a three-word title) is quite difficult to fit into a horizontal space such as that which exists under many header blocks. Conversely, a short set of five elements can appear distinctly bleak if given significant space in a side block.

Top Navigation

As has been briefly mentioned, navigation positioned immediately following a site header is a popular option, and is most effective with smaller groups of primary navigation. Given that the aspect ratio of monitors leaves them wider than they are tall, using vertical screen real estate should not be considered lightly and stacking primary and secondary navigation is a bad idea on all but the most terse of sites.

That said, average screen resolution is increasing and anecdotal evidence suggests that a growing number of users tend to browse simultaneously with multiple windows, each sized to a portrait orientation, rather than a single, maximized window. Also, users are not completely averse to vertical scrolling, and adding 20px for your second-level navigation may, at times, be a lesser evil than removing 150px from the side of your template.

A combination of top and left navigation is a regularly employed solution for navigation that runs two or more levels deep, providing some clarity between levels.

Bottom Navigation

Generally, navigation positioned at the bottom of the screen is a bad idea. To circumvent the risk of it slipping off-screen, the usual methods of implementation use frames in otherwise avoidable situations, or DHTML that is far less (or not at all) reliable in older browsers. It is, though, sensible to replicate top or side navigation in a text format at the footer of your site.

Many users of the Web are accustomed to seeking links to content at the top or on the left-hand side of the screen. Consequently, it is unwise to fight the expectations of users about the behavior of your site and the positioning of crucial elements.

Left Navigation

Along with top navigation, links in left-hand sidebars account for many of the layouts on the Web today. The inclination towards this orientation can be attributed to a number of factors including:

- Priority of location: Elements towards the top-left of the browser space attract immediate attention from most visitors. Navigation beginning below this point and running down the left-hand side is often next in line after the high-priority position and header block.

- Real estate: The aspect ratio of computer screens provides more horizontal space than vertical. This makes for easier use of a column devoted to navigation than a thin block potentially wasting valuable vertical space.

- Never requires horizontal scrolling: Even if your layout pushes out beyond the browser-width of your visitors, a left-hand navigation block will always start on screen, even if horizontal scrolling is required to read text or reach other items.

- User inertia: Your layout is instantly assisted by your elements being close to where users would expect to find them. Navigation on the left side of your layout, therefore, has an advantage stemming from its existing popularity.

Right Navigation

With visitor attention usually greatest in the top-left corner and less so on the right-hand side of the page, right-hand navigation is rarely advisable. When viewed at a lower resolution, some poorly designed sites with this layout can lose their navigation off-screen. With simple sites it can be quite successful and give more prominence to content, as shown by Toop&Toop:

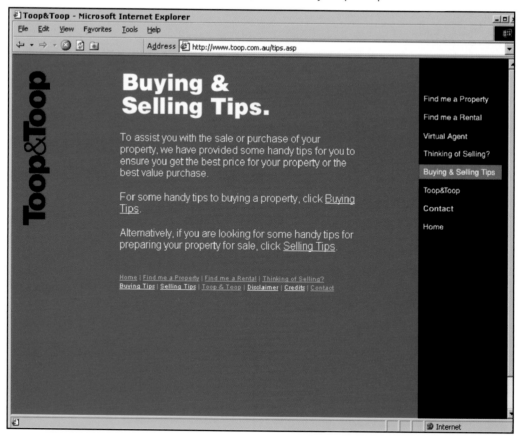

Home Pages or Front Doors

The home pages or front doors of a site, such as the examples presented below, are your chance to make a solid first impression on your visitors. As such, they provide an excellent opportunity to showcase the point of difference of your business, the best-selling products from your catalog or featured members of your community. It is possible to create a home page that can, within seconds, give a user an accurate idea of the strengths and qualities of your organization:

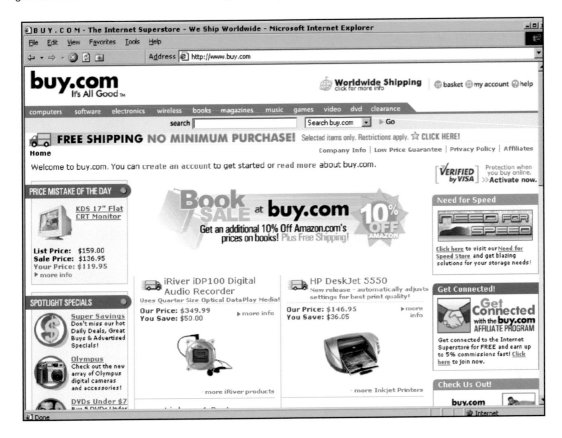

The majority of site front doors are composed of introductory material and special promotions, and your layout is often determined by the size of these elements.

As an example, consider a front door requiring a large introduction (composed of a tagline, small image, and brief paragraph of text), two small promotions, and a "Top ten products" listing of titles. Assuming that the positioning of primary navigation has already been arranged within your shell design, you will be deciding how to divide the remaining space. Analyzing each element is straightforward:

- The introduction: The size of this element immediately suggests that it requires a broad block. With the number of subitems, however, it is likely that this introduction is relatively fluid and could also fill a narrower, but taller space. It would be best suited to either the wider column of an unequally spaced two-column content layout, or either column of a 50:50 two-column split.

- Two promotions: Smaller promotions could easily be stacked in the narrower column of a two-column layout. Alternatively, they could be positioned adjacent to one another in a wider column. Given their size, though, they would not be best placed each in their own column if the columns were fifty percent of the total layout.

- Top ten listing: A listing that includes product thumbnails and brief descriptions could realistically only fit in a wider column, but in this example, we are considering a listing of ten titles only. This would be appropriately positioned within either a narrower column, or either of two equally sized columns. In the narrower column, most titles would wrap to a new line and the resulting element size would be proportionately longer than wide.

This information should point you towards a preferred layout option. The first element is suited to a 50:50 two-column layout, or the wider of, perhaps, an 80:20 layout. The second two elements would be best placed either adjacent in a wider column, or stacked in a narrower option. Their lack of favor for the 50:50 option goes some way to eliminating it as a possibility. The listing could work within a 50:50 layout, or in the narrow column of an 80:20 layout.

From this, it would be worth investigating the 80:20 layout at the following approximate positioning:

A variety of non-standard layouts can be known to work. These two screenshots may provide you with inspiration for front-door layouts:

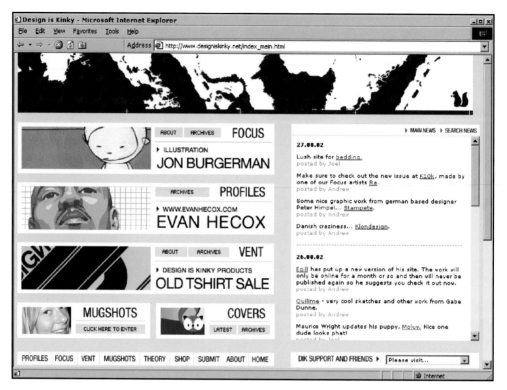

Content Pages

Composed mostly of text and non-actionable images, content pages require clean presentation to allow your users to focus on the content itself. Images or side notes are nested within with a left or right alignment, forcing text to wrap around.

If your shell design does not use three columns, and situates the content in the center, then splitting your content into 80:20 columns might be viable. The narrower of the columns can be a useful location for such tools as article rating information, printing options, and features such as "E-mail this to a friend".

An example of a site showing the third column being used for related information (*news.bbc.co.uk*) is shown opposite:

Product Pages

More than almost any other type of page, a product template needs to be very action-oriented. Users are there to research, hopefully to select an item, and then complete a checkout or inquiry process. Related information, including provision for the user to make an inquiry, needs to be close by.

The layout you use will depend on the information and options presented for each product, as well as the importance of graphical support. Promoting the sale of a house online, for example, is likely to be backed by a small photo gallery, virtual tour, and other information. A clothing store will have color and size options for much of its catalog.

The examples below may give you ideas worth experimenting with for your product templates:

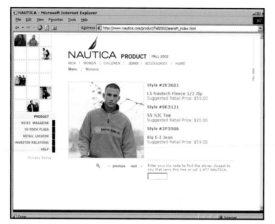

General Layout

Applying to shell, front door, content, and product templates are a number of layouts with which you will find it useful to familiarize yourself. As with a lot of design issues, it is not always a simple concept to adopt, but with reasoning, inspiration, and practice, you can (at the very least) improve your work.

Single Column

Single column layouts, while extraordinarily simple to create, are somewhat rare. They are best avoided when one has to contend with multiple levels of navigation, related information, or supplementary promotions. For very straightforward sites with navigation placed in a block at the top of the screen, they should be considered.

As shown in the example below, some single-column layouts use blocks of color or images to imply the structure that can be lacking when content is arranged within a single column:

Two Columns

Another simple layout is that which uses a second column. Generally this added column is on the left-hand side of the page, and populated with navigational elements, or on the right-hand side, and filled with related information, search functions, and advertising.

Two-column layouts have been one of the more popular layouts employed online due to their ability to effectively separate groups of content. Most often, one of the columns is narrower and leaves the wider region open for content. At times, though, a 50:50 two-column layout can balance content or product information with extensive navigation.

The examples of two-column layouts that follow may provide you with some inspiration:

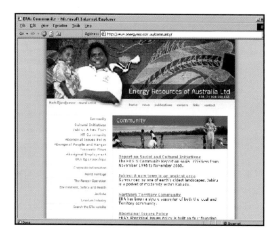

Three Columns

More complex sites with extended navigational hierarchies and cross-linking frequently require a greater separation of elements than can be offered by a two-column layout. Here, a third column is an excellent choice.

It does, however, bring an additional degree of complexity and thus opportunity for problems. Unfortunately, this is especially an issue when using CSS for layout instead of HTML tables.

The use of the three columns in this type of layout commonly falls to navigation, content, and then related information. It is also, though rarely, used for navigation, a second level of navigation, and then content.

At times a third column features expendable elements in a technique discussed within the next few paragraphs.

Four Columns

A fourth column is sometimes used on a site front door where the components of your layout are brief introductory portions promoting sections of your site. For content templates featuring substantial blocks of text and images, the complexity of a fourth column is something to steer clear of. The same goes when designing for users more likely to be using older hardware and a lower resolution; they will not have the screen real estate available for too many columns.

The front door and section doorways of *Salon.com* are examples of four-column layouts, as is The New York Times:

Sacrificial Columns

A column with elements of low priority can be considered expendable and is a useful means of fitting everything into your layout without losing focus on key items. It is a technique that can also give an enhanced feel to visitors with a higher resolution, without ruining the experience for those with a lower resolution.

Sacrificial columns are usually adopted with 2-4 column layouts, and are always the right-most column in your layout. The theory goes that comparably expendable content sits in the sacrificial column and is visible to users browsing at a higher resolution (or simply with a wider browser window). To those with lower resolutions, however, it is the first column to be lost off-screen and require horizontal scrolling to view. This is a less than critical issue considering the nature of the off-screen material.

Items likely to be found in sacrificial columns include related topics, tertiary promotions, third-party advertisements, and low-priority tools such as the ability to rate an article, or e-mail an article to a friend. None of these items are usually vital to core site goals.

Given that this approach is forward thinking (average user resolution is increasing), yet accommodating, there are virtually no disadvantages. The only thing to keep in mind is the bandwidth usage of adding extra information to the screen. If your templates are taking too long to download, you should consider losing some of the lower priority components.

The sites below both employ sacrificial columns. In the first, the final column is used for an advertisement. In the second, it is used for a tertiary promotion:

Alignment

As important as consideration of element priorities and layout options are, a template layout can still be left far short of its best if items are misaligned. Ignored or poorly planned alignment is close to, if not actually, the greatest failing of many sites not designed by professional designers (and even some that are).

The components of your layout, from the header items, through features and content, to the footer, should work together to meet the aims of your site. Misaligned elements distract from these goals and present an amateur appearance to your visitors.

The advantages of a well-aligned layout includes giving a cleaner and more relaxed first impression, and making it easier for strong visual clues such as changes in color and shape to draw the eye of each user.

The best way to understand non-ideal alignment is to witness it in action:

The overall feel of this design could be improved with minor adjustments to the layout as per the alterations below. These include alterations to fit content into three distinct columns, minor tweaks to align the boxes in the left and right sidebars, and shifting header elements to give a solid opening for alignment. The content under the Best Value subtitle has been adjusted to wrap at the width of the product information to give better clarity to the Add-to-cart and Wish List action areas:

Naturally well-aligned sites such as the following exude a professional feel that give visitors an impression of quality, care, and trustworthiness that would be desirable response goals for many sites on the Internet:

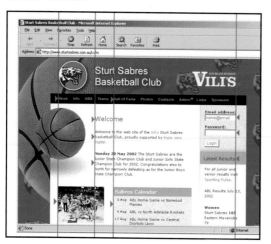 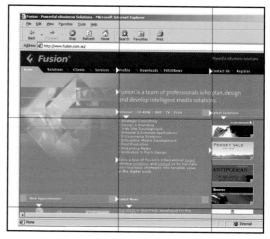

While horizontal alignment is particularly important, vertical positioning is a simple investment with substantial returns. The opportunities for vertical alignment, while fewer than those in the horizontal counterpart, do exist across the columns of the average layout. For example, aligning the top of left-navigation with the heading of a content page is a simple habit to get into.

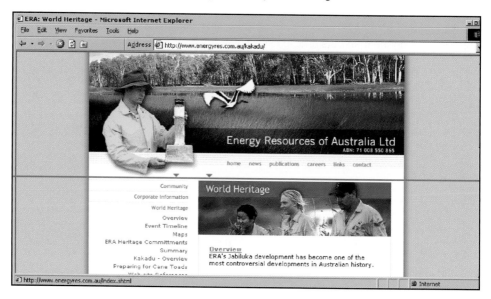

Where possible, your logo, tagline, navigation, and other items should be placed equidistantly from either the top of the page or the divider that separates the header block from the rest of your content. Navigation and branding elements in the demonstration below are spaced evenly from a dividing line:

Essentially, the key to good alignment is maintaining a visual grid through the design and implementation processes. This visual grid should be composed of imaginary lines crossing your layout, both vertically and horizontally. While in some cases these primary alignment guides can be equally spaced, it is not normally required, and at times can appear stilted.

The Design Process

During the design process, ensuring that your elements are aligned to a visual grid is simplified with the use of tools within your preferred graphics application. Photoshop, as an example, provides layout guides and grids for exactly this purpose.

Layout Guides

Layout guides are specific to each of your images in applications such as Photoshop, Fireworks, and Paint Shop Pro, making them an outstanding assistant in the creation of a constant visual grid for your shell and content layout. The guides themselves are not part of your image itself and are not shown in the final image or when printed; they float above and merely provide anchoring points for your layers and selection tools.

Creating a guide is a simple process that begins with enabling rulers within your document. Rulers can be quickly toggled in Photoshop using the CTRL+R keyboard shortcut (Apple+R on a Mac), or via the View menu. The same works in Corel PhotoPaint, while CTRL+ALT+R works in Paint Shop Pro and Fireworks MX.

Once the rulers are visible, in Photoshop you can create horizontal and vertical guides by clicking the respective ruler and dragging out into the working space of your image. Holding the SHIFT key "snaps" the guide being dragged to one of the tick marks on the appropriate ruler. Holding the ALT key allows you to drag a horizontal guide from the vertical ruler, and vice versa. To place a guide at a predefined location, use the *View > New Guide...* menu option. In PhotoPaint, the *View > Guidelines setup* opens a dialog that lets you add more, or delete multiple horizontal and vertical guidelines at the same time. In Fireworks and Paint Shop Pro, the guidelines dialog only allows you to change colors or delete all guides.

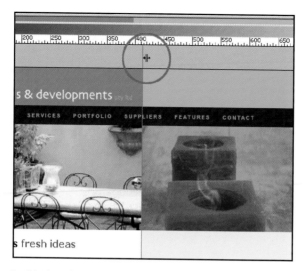

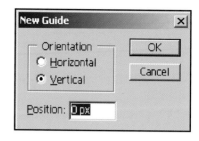

The double-header arrow cursor near a guide in Photoshop

The *View > New Guide* dialog.

To move a guide from its current position, you can mouse near its position while using the move tool (keyboard shortcut: V), then click-and-drag when the cursor changes to the double-headed arrow. Alternatively (when using any tool except for hand, zoom, or slice) holding the CTRL key when near a guide will change the cursor to the double-headed arrow.

In PhotoPaint, the cursor when shifting a guide is a small pointing hand and requires no keystroke modifiers. In Fireworks, it is a double-headed arrow, but again requires no keystrokes. In Paint Shop Pro, a crosshair cursor allows you to move intersecting guides, or double-click the point of intersection to adjust them with a specific pixel value.

Once in place, dragging it out of the workspace and releasing can remove a guide in Photoshop and PhotoPaint. Toggling visibility of your layout guides is done with the keyboard shortcut CTRL+' in Photoshop.

When working, you will more often than not want to have the snap-to-guides setting on. You should ensure that your alignment is pixel-perfect, and not rely on approximate judgments. In Fireworks, CTRL+SHFT+; toggles snapping, while in PhotoPaint, it is CTRL+;.

Layout guides provide an excellent means by which you can enact the final cut-up of your Photoshop documents into the JPG and GIF component images that will be included with your HTML templates.

Grids

Unlike guides, grids in Photoshop are a global setting and apply to all of your images. In Corel PhotoPaint, though, they are set on a per-document basis. The settings of your grid can be changed under the relevant section in the *Edit > Preferences* dialog. As with layout guides, you can arrange for your select tools and layers to snap to grid lines. Also, the keyboard shortcut ALT+CTRL+' provides a quick way of toggling the visibility of the layout grid in Photoshop, while CTRL+' does the same in PhotoPaint.

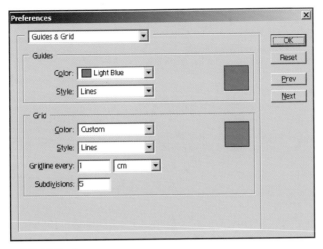

Photoshop's Guides and Grid Preferences.

View > Snap To menu location.

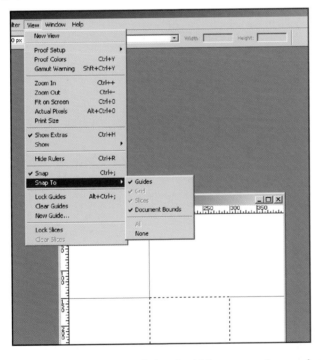

When you base a layout around equally spaced visual grid lines, a workspace function such as Photoshop's grid can be useful.

Implementation

Where layout guides help during the design process, HTML tables or concise CSS layout code makes it a little harder to get things wrong during implementation.

One point, however, where care must be taken is when using nested tables. If using multiple rows within a single table, the column widths are inherited from row to row, and alignment tends to occur naturally. With nested tables the same is not necessarily true, and even with defined column widths, improperly sized visual elements (usually images) can force columns out of the width you may have otherwise set.

Once knee-deep in HTML and without your layout guides, you will need to rely on table borders, particular calculations, and personal judgment to guarantee that your headings, text blocks, navigation, promotions, and other visual elements are accurately aligned. This alignment is a vital piece of the puzzle that may have otherwise troubled you in producing a professional and readable web site.

Layout with Tables

For a while now, web page layout has been accomplished for the majority of sites using HTML tables. The comparable ease of use, and subsequent popularity, of WYSIWYG editors with their ability to automatically generate such tables has made table-based layouts no less attractive.

A two-column layout can be created using tables as per the code below:

```
<table>

<tr>

<td>Left column</td>

<td>Right column</td>

</tr>

</table>
```

While this looks harmless enough, customizing the padding and borders of these two columns immediately increases the complexity of the code. This is especially the case where the padding or border values need to be set independently for each side of the column boxes. Most often, nested tables will be required, and bring with them code bloat and confusion.

Regardless, there is reasonable rendering accuracy across new and old browsers. This is useful in that content in a right column stays in the right column, unlike the situation with CSS where a `<div>` positioned as a right column degrades in older browsers to appear in a marked-up sequence. For example, A List Apart viewed in a browser with CSS support:

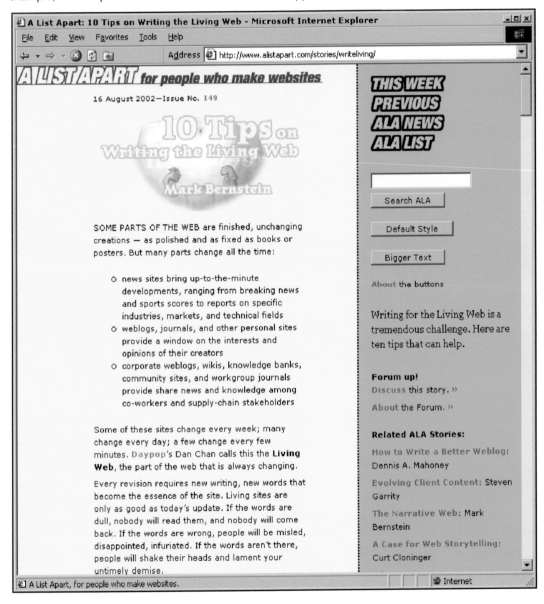

In an older browser, the CSS layout is lost, and the right column moves…

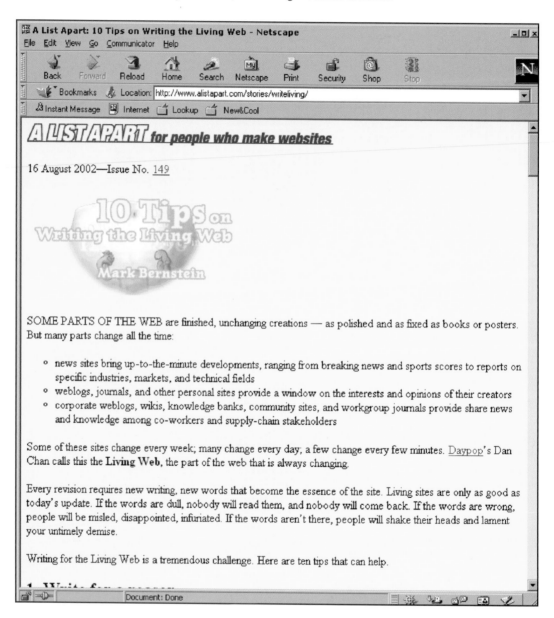

…to the bottom of the page and after the article since the article div appeared first in the page markup.

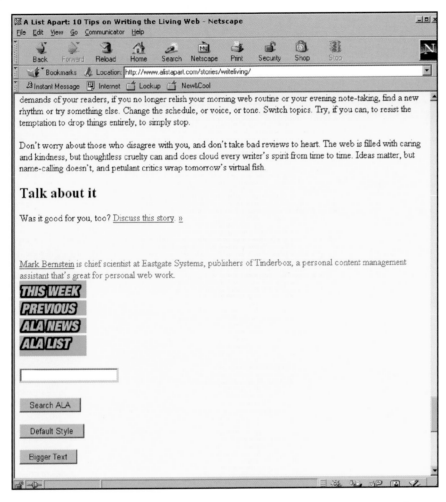

The disadvantages with table-based layout, however, include code bloat. If we extend layout tables to include non-uniform borders and padding, we need a substantial amount of extra code. Such code is also difficult to maintain, and for new developers to get up to speed with.

An example of a nested table required to give cell padding is provided below:

```
<table border="0" cellpadding="0" cellspacing="0" width="300">
<tr>
<td width="10">
  <img src="/images/spacer.gif" width="10" height="1" border="0">
</td>
```

```
<td>Content.</td>
<td width="40">
  <img src="/images/spacer.gif" width="40" height="1" border="0">
</td>
</tr>
</table>
```

Adding borders gives another dimension of complexity on top of this. For purposes of comparison, this padding can be emulated with CSS as follows:

```
<div style="padding-left:10px; padding-right:40px;">Content.</div>
```

Layout with CSS

Layout with CSS is accomplished using a series of `<div>` tags that are positioned using position, display, and float attributes.

The following code within an HTML page shows a `<div>`:

```
<div id="ninoheader">
  <h1>Nino's Shoes</h1>
  <p><a href="/store/" title="The Store">Buy</a><br>
<a href="/score/" title="The Score">Action</a></p>
</div>
```

This code demonstrates the styling applied within an external stylesheet:

```
#ninoheader {position: relative ;
             margin-right: 0px ;
             margin-left: 100px ;
             top: 0px ;
             padding: 5px 40px 5px 30px ;
             background-color:#cccccc;}
```

This code combination presents the following raw page:

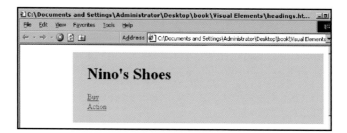

With the ability of CSS to locate elements with precise absolute positioning, and flexible relative positioning, the nested tables and spacer GIFs of table-based layouts are no longer required. This removes much of the unnecessary HTML that proves confusing to maintain, and provides only a marginal increase in download time.

As has been previously outlined, however, this layout loses its applied positioning in browsers that do not support CSS, and instead stack vertically in the order of their inclusion within the HTML page.

One of the other caveats to CSS-only layouts relates to all the quirks the different browsers exhibit when you use otherwise valid CSS. Throw Navigator 4.x into the mix, and you'll likely pull your hair out before you get a complete design. But fear not, there are some very kind, very dedicated, very frazzled folks on the web who have experienced most of these bugs and found ways around them, resulting in sample layouts that you can use as a base for some of your designs:

- Glish.com, by Eric Costello *http://glish.com/css/*

  Gives sample layouts in two-, three-, and four-columns, including the ALA layout. Each of his pages has the HTML/CSS source of the page at the bottom of the page. It's also worth looking at *http://glish.com/css/hacks.asp*, a collection of hacks used to get around some rendering quirks in various browsers. Note these are hacks, so they aren't always pretty. And they don't address all the bugs out there.

- Box Lessons by Owen Briggs *http://thenoodleincident.com/tutorials/box_lesson/*

  Samples and tutorials on how to understand and apply the "box model" of CSS, as well as hacks, handy links, and some commentary. And the color scheme is friendly to those of us with raster burn.

- BlueRobot by Rob Chandanais *http://bluerobot.com/web/layouts/*

  The Layout Reservoir has some sample two- and three-column layouts that you may freely mangle. Just don't steal his homepage design, it happens too often as it is.

Best Practice

As we've seen in the course of this chapter, there are many issues to be aware of when laying out your page. The key points we looked at are as follows:

- Identify your elements for each fresh design or redesign

- Group and prioritize them

- Use this information to select a layout, and then work with that until you find something that works well

- Remember that color and location can help to group elements

- Where possible, know the average browsing capacity and preferences of your audience

- Choose a layout that will best meet the preferences of as many users as possible

- Consider changing your layout slightly where the requirements of templates differ, but maintain a uniform shell throughout

- Never disregard alignment; it can do much to enhance your design and layout

- Always use guides in your image editor

5

Layout

6

- The essential formats
- DPI issues
- When not to use bitmaps

Author: Dave Gibbons

File Formats and File Sizes

So now you know how to make the graphics usable and attractive. Here's where we get into a little of the techie stuff - nothing too esoteric, just the important technical choices that make graphics more usable. How do you make web graphics download faster, for example? This chapter shows why it's important to choose particular file formats for specific purposes. A single format does not work for all uses - not yet, anyway.

We'll look at the main two file formats you'll want to use on the Web: GIF and JPEG. The principal points of discussion will include:

- The limitations of each format

- When to use each

- The effects of compression, both on file size and picture quality

- The introduction of a third format, PNG

- Issues involved in scanning images for the Web

The Essential Formats: GIF and JPEG

All graphical browsers support GIF and JPEG image formats. While there are literally dozens of graphic formats we could discuss here, most notably a newer format called PNG ("ping"), GIF and JPEG are the foundations of web graphical presentation today.

6

If you're interested in the history of these formats or their more obscure traits (for example, did you know GIF uses Lempel-Ziv compression? Do you care?), you can find the spec at *http://www.w3.org/Graphics/GIF/spec-gif89a.txt*. This chapter discusses only what you'll need to know to get the most out of them in the real world - or its online equivalent.

Both GIF and JPEG are bitmap formats (also called "raster" formats), which as you probably know means they are made up of pixels ("picture elements", which essentially means colored dots). By contrast, vector graphical formats, like SVG ("scalable vector graphics", mostly used in conjunction with XML applications) and Flash, are made up of **instructions** instead of pixels. As we'll see in *Chapter 8*, with a vector format you can draw a large circle on the screen with just a few instructions to the rendering software (how big the circle is, where it is positioned on the screen, the width of the line, and any color instructions), and therefore just a few bytes of information. The same large circle in a bitmap format would include pixels for each point in the circle and more pixels for colors inside or outside the circle - potentially a huge amount of data for the same circle on the screen. If the vector-based circle got bigger, the file size would stay pretty much the same, since you'd only be changing the single instruction that told the browser its size. If the bitmap circle grew, though, so would the file size because you'd be adding more and more pixels.

File size is one of the major considerations in creating usable web graphics. Even if you're enjoying a lightning-fast LAN or other broadband connection, your web work needs to accommodate the majority of web users who still use plain-old dialup or cutting-edge wireless connections - all of which currently work at a relatively pokey pace at or under 56Kbps. For example, a 200K graphic that takes a second or two to show up with your broadband connection would take about 30 seconds to download on a 56K connection. If that graphic is your logo, it's more than a little annoying for the user. If it's your main menu, however, a 30-second lag is quite annoying, possibly unusable. As a rule of thumb, in fact, a page should be able to load within a minute.

File Size	500Kbps speed (broadband)	56Kbps modem	28Kbps modem
I MB (medium-sized Flash animation)	16 seconds	143 seconds	286 seconds
200KB (very large graphic)	3 seconds	29 seconds	57 seconds
20 KB (standard-size graphic)	<1 second	3 seconds	6 seconds

Both GIF and JPEG use compression mechanisms that cut down file size. Both are universally supported bitmap formats - at least they're universally supported on desktop graphical browsers. So why choose one or the other? Because even though they're technically similar, they're designed for very different applications. The following table illustrates the principal differences between JPEG and GIF:

	Color palette	Compression	Animation	Transparency
JPEG	Virtually unlimited (24-bit is supported by most browsers)	Lossy; highly customizable	None	None
GIF	Limited to 256 colors (8-bit)	Lossless; simple run-length encoding	Handled by embedding multiple pictures into one file	Available by setting a transparent color

JPEG

Conventional wisdom says JPEG is exclusively for photos and GIF is for everything else. The "P" in JPEG is, in fact, "Photographic" (the "Joint Photographic Experts Group" designed the format). Digitizing photographs is a very different process from digitizing words or line drawings. Photographs are usually made up of continuous tones without very sharp distinctions between objects. The flow of color change across the skin in a shadow under a person's nose, for example, is not a perfect outline of the nose. As you see in the example below, you can blur much of the information in a photograph and still recognize the image.

JPEG compression is very flexible. These JPEGs look very similar at first glance, but the one on the left is 487Kb while the one on the right is 48Kb.

JPEG's approach is called "lossy" compression, because you literally lose some of the picture's information when you compress it with JPEG. Don't panic when you hear that the compression is "lossy", though. What you "lose" is minute variations in color, which are replaced with colors that meet somewhere between the original colors. As you see in the example, the tightly compressed version on the right loses only a bit of detail in very busy and colorful elements, like the man's tie, his jacket, and the wrinkles on the bridge of his nose.

6

The following close-ups on the same part of the image illustrate the difference in quality as we zoom in:

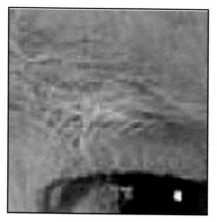 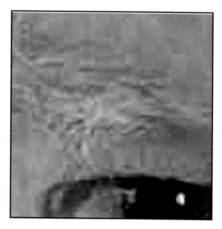

Words, like the ones you're reading now at 1270 dots per inch (dpi) or those you see on your monitor at something like 96 ppi (pixels per inch) on Windows or 72 on Mac, require sharp boundaries and little or no loss. You can do simple edge smoothing on text (anti-aliasing, which blurs the text a bit), but you can't compromise more than a pixel or two along the edges of the letters without the effect becoming very noticeable. If you compress a paragraph of text with JPEG, it usually becomes unreadable:

Quelque 10 millions d'Américains surfent sur internet sans fil

RESTON, Virginie (Reuters) - Près de 10 millions d'Américains consultent leurs e-mails ou recherchent des informations sur internet à partir de leur mobile ou d'un ordinateur portable, une étude de l'institut de recherche ComScore Media Metrix.

Cinq des 19,1 millions de propriétaires d'un ordinateur portable et 5,8 millions des 67,2 milli d'utilisateurs de mobiles ont un accès à internet sans fil, indique l'institut qui précise que le no est ramené dans l'absolu à 9,9 millions du fait des personnes utilisant les deux moyens de connexion, soit 11% des adeptes du sans fil aux Etats-Unis.

In this example, the original graphic only had black pixels and white pixels, with very sharp edges. JPEG compression, which, as we mentioned before, smoothes out very busy objects and hard edges, tries to blend the hard edges of the black letters into the white background. The result, as you see, is as muddy as a page that looks like it has been photocopied too many times. As a rule of thumb, JPEG is great for pictures, but not good at all for text, cartoons, and other graphics that require hard edges.

Enter GIF, a format that uses "lossless" compression:

> ## Quelque 10 millions d'Américains surfent sur internet sans fil
>
> RESTON, Virginie (Reuters) - Près de 10 millions d'Américains consultent leurs e-mails ou recherchent des informations sur internet à partir de leur mobile ou d'un ordinateur portable, selon une étude de l'institut de recherche ComScore Media Metrix.
>
> Cinq des 19,1 millions de propriétaires d'un ordinateur portable et 5,8 millions des 67,2 millions d'utilisateurs de mobiles ont un accès à internet sans fil, indique l'institut qui précise que le nombre est ramené dans l'absolu à 9,9 millions du fait des personnes utilisant les deux moyens de connexion, soit 11% des adeptes du sans fil aux Etats-Unis.

Interestingly, the JPEG image of the text takes up 44KB, while the GIF image is only 6KB, so as well as being clearer it is also smaller and naturally a quicker download - an example of the right image format for the right purpose.

GIF

For any image that requires clearly defined boundaries and flat color, including text, cartoons, drawings, screenshots, and computer-generated graphics, GIF is a natural choice - up to a point. GIF has its limitations as well, particularly in that it can only display images that contain 256 colors or less. This is why GIF isn't the best choice for photographs, even though it's capable of storing photographs. Still, it's rare that a graphic on the Web (apart from a photograph) requires anything near 256 discrete colors - at least for now. If you've created an intricate computer graphic with a thousand discrete colors, you have two choices: make it a JPEG or use the "dithering" feature in your graphics software to cut down the colors to a GIF-safe 256.

Dithering reduces the number of colors in a graphic by picking dominant colors and filling pixels that have similar tones with those colors. For example, if you have a smooth gradient fill from red to blue (see below), you'll have some pixels in the middle that are 50% red/50% blue (standard purple), while all the intervening steps are odd numbers like 21% red/79% blue. Depending on how you dither the picture, you might see bands of different colors (red, maroon, purple, indigo, blue), no change at all, or anything in between.

No dithering (469 KB):

Ordered dithering, optimized (24KB):

Error diffusion dithering, adaptive (36KB):

Ordered palette dithering, uniform (8 KB):

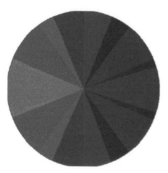

Let's look at the first three images in close-up, to see the differences:

No dithering:

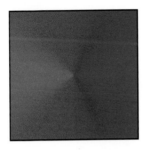

Ordered dithering:

Error diffusion dithering:

Ordered palette dithering:

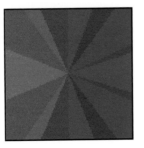

It should be noted that in most situations, dithering doesn't cause such stark contrasts.

So what if you want to use a photograph with a GIF-specific feature like animation or transparency? You'll have to use your graphics software (see the *Chapter 7* on graphics software) to dither the photo down to 256 colors or fewer, but that should be acceptable for most photos after a bit of experimentation:

The GIF on the left uses a standard ordered palette, resulting in a very messy file (176KB in this example). The one on the right uses "optimized" dithering, giving us a reasonably clean picture but a much larger file (483KB in this example). Compare this to the compressed JPEG we saw earlier, which was 48KB.

Coming Soon: PNG ("ping")

In the technological bullpen is a new graphics standard that will, according to its proponents, change everything (not unlike other "this will change everything" technologies like XML, WAP, and Bluetooth). PNG is similar to GIF in that it offers lossless compression, animation, and transparency, but PNG does each better. Much better.

PNG's promise includes:

- **Progressive display**, which means a graphic can be shown in layers or increasing clarity, starting with a general idea of the final picture and gradually adding more layers of detail (this feature is also available in GIF, where it is known as interlacing)

- **Advanced transparency options** that don't rely on the GIF technique of "erasing" specific colors. This is a major problem with transparent GIF files. If you set "white" as your transparent color in a GIF file, for example, you might end up with a person with transparent eyes or seemingly random bits of transparency where individual white pixels become transparent. With PNG, however, you can define a region as transparent regardless of what colors would be "erased" by this process.

- Lossless compression

- Very good compression (up to twice as good as GIF)

- Virtually unlimited colors (up to 48-bit color, referred to as "True Color" because it is as good as the human eye can perceive - better, in fact)

The main attraction for designers will probably be PNG's JPEG-style nearly unlimited color palette (up to 48-bit color), knocking down one of the main drawbacks of GIF and positioning PNG as a reasonable replacement for both GIF and JPEG. The consensus in the industry is that PNG will be a natural successor to GIF, but that JPEG's natural kinship with photographs will keep it in the web design arena.

At this writing, the newest versions of Internet Explorer and Netscape support PNG to varying degrees (see *http://www.libpng.org/pub/png/pngapbr.html* for details), with full support expected in the near future. Older browsers, like Internet Explorer 4, can't display PNG at all, while even IE 6 can't display many PNG images with complex transparency. This means virtually none of your users will be able to see advanced PNG images in their browsers. Most bitmap graphics applications, however, can already open, manipulate, and create PNG files, though you'll have to check the application's documentation to see if it supports all of PNG's more advanced features. In practical terms, this means you should be prepared to incorporate PNG into your graphics repertoire, and you can probably start playing with it using the graphics application you already own, but it will be a few years before the majority of web users have browsers that are compatible with PNG.

The Two Big DPI Issues

When working with graphics for the Web, people need to keep in mind two issues of resolution (commonly expressed as "dpi" or "dots per inch"). The first issue is the resolution of the source graphic. The second is the size you want it to appear on the screen. Both factors are commonly misunderstood.

The resolution of the source graphic is controlled by the graphics or scanning program you use to create or manipulate it. For the sake of illustration, we'll assume you have a new 1200 dpi scanner and you want the best possible picture it can deliver, which you will then publish to the Web. Even though it sounds counterintuitive, the best picture you can create with this scanner is not 1200 dpi - at least not for web delivery. For the Web, you'll probably want to scan any picture you use at 100dpi or so. Here's an example of why scanning at a very high resolution is counterproductive:

In this example, let's say you scan a 2-inch (~5 cm) square at the maximum resolution of the scanner: 1200 dpi. Mathematics tells us the resulting graphic contains 5,760,000 pixels (less with compression, but we're considering the worst-case scenario). Each of those pixels could be anything from 1 bit black-and-white (720,000 bytes) at one extreme to 48-bit color (34,560,000 bytes) at the other, or even higher. What happens when we display those graphics in a web browser? In addition to having to wait forever to download them (even the small example is a very large file at 720K, and 34.5MB for the 48-bit color file is ridiculous), we get another surprise: we don't see a 2-inch square graphic any more. Now we see our graphic exploded to 24 inches or so, depending on the resolution of the monitor:

6

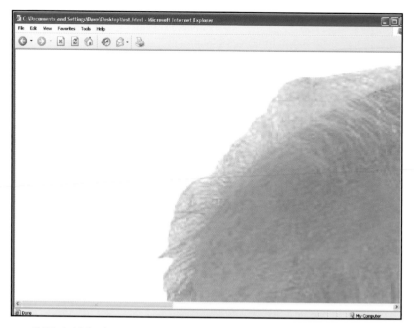

What went wrong? We told the browser to show our 2-inch square, right? Well, no. There are two rules to keep in mind when putting bitmap graphics online.

Rule #1: Monitors (and, by extension, browsers) don't know anything about dots per inch, they only know about pixels.

If you put a 2400-pixel-wide picture on a 100 dpi monitor, for example, the monitor will show you one of its pixels for each dot in the original, therefore the picture shows at 24 inches across. What you really want is not a 2400-pixel-wide graphic, then. You really want one that is maybe 200 pixels wide (assuming 100 dpi in this case). You can shrink your graphic in a graphics program or use a more efficient resolution in the scanning software, but whatever method you choose, you'll want to make the source file **as close as possible to the desired output size.**

In addition to controlling the size of the original graphic, we need to decide how big we want the graphic to appear in the browser. Here, you use the `<img>` tag in the HTML:

```
<img src="location/filename" width="X pixels" height="Y pixels">
```

The most important thing to keep in mind here is:

Rule #2: The width and height factors in the `<img>` tag are **screen pixels**, not pixels in the original graphic.

With our example, now that we've got a 200-pixel graphic instead of the 2400-pixel monstrosity, if we wanted a 1-to-1 relationship between pixels in the new graphic file and pixels on the screen we'd use this tag:

```
<img src="location/filename" width="200" height="200">
```

Will this give us a 2-inch graphic on the screen? Probably not, but it will be close enough for most desktop monitors. Screen sizes vary widely, from the 2-inch quarter-VGA screens on PDAs to giant 38-inch conference room monitors and beyond in both directions, and most can be set to different resolutions. On some monitors, each horizontal inch shows 60 pixels; some 70, 80, 96, 100, 125, or just about any other number. 2 inches, then, could be 120 pixels or 250 pixels, or something else. Can we ask for 2 inches of screen real estate? No (at least not until we get into some more advanced CSS). Remember Rule #1: Monitors (and, by extension, browsers) don't know about dpi, they only know about pixels. We can ask for a certain number of pixels, but not a certain amount of space.

So, remembering Rule #2, we need to set up our `<img>` tag to show the appropriate amount of screen space, regardless of the original image's resolution. These values should match but they don't necessarily have to match - you could go wild and squeeze that earlier 24-inch-wide example into a 2-inch space, but that would be a huge waste of space and bandwidth and would probably look horrible to boot.

Using our 200-by-200-pixel image and the corresponding 200-by-200-pixel image tag, we see what we intended: a roughly two-inch square.

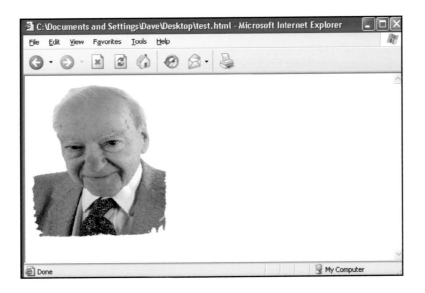

Know When Not to Use Bitmaps

At the beginning of this chapter, we discussed some of the disadvantages of using bitmapped graphics versus vector graphics - primarily size, but also quality. When the computer is figuring out how to draw a line or a letter rather than using a pre-drawn bitmap, the quality is often noticeably better.

For text, use bitmaps sparingly if at all. Your company logo is probably a bitmap, which is natural, but unless you have some particularly earth-shattering effects to apply to headings and menus, stick with plain text. In fact, you can apply some pretty earth-shattering effects (including simple things like shadows and fonts) using cascading stylesheets (CSS). See *Chapter 3* for more details on how to use text effectively.

Two other areas where bitmaps can frequently be replaced are in animation and mouseover effects. CSS is an excellent option for mousover effects, as is JavaScript/JScript. See if you can achieve the same results with Flash (a vector-based program that can open up endless possibilities for relatively little bandwidth). If you're animating something that has to be a bitmap, like a photograph, Flash won't save you any space and may even add overhead, but for most other applications it offers more flexibility than script languages for similar bandwidth. Of course, adding proprietary content to a site introduces the problem of users who don't have the right plugin for their browser, so in the end you may be better served by sticking to open standards like CSS and JavaScript/JScript rather than adding Flash.

Summary

GIF, JPEG, and soon PNG are the staples of web graphics, but they're not for all applications. JPEG is excellent for photographs; GIF and PNG for just about everything else. All types of bitmaps are notoriously susceptible to bloating, which adversely affects the download speed of your pages. When you use bitmaps, remember that the concept of "dots per inch" has a unique meaning in the browser world. Browsers don't know the original size of the source graphic, they only understand the instructions in the `<img>` tag. They display graphics to the specifications of the `<img>` tag, even if it tells the browser to stretch or squeeze the graphic. This behavior can be exploited, stretching single-pixel graphics into lines, bars, and rectangles. There are other strategies for reducing bandwidth, including replacing bitmaps with text and CSS, as we saw in *Chapter 3*, or with Flash or other vector graphics, as we shall see in *Chapter 8*.

7

- Basic optimization
- Image slicing
- Web graphics packages

Author: Adrian Roselli

Graphics Applications

Now that we've worked our way through a number of design techniques, we need to know how to take our work and get it ready for the Web. We've touched on some of the graphics applications techniques here and there so far, but now is our opportunity to sit down and explore our options for outputting our designs.

There are graphics tools out there for nearly any platform and any need, and all you have to do is spend some time searching on the Web. Some are very specialized - they may only act as image viewers, or only handle color palettes, or just do animation, but more likely than not you can find a tool that will perform some function that is not in your favorite tool, which is why looking at the tools in this chapter will help you see a little more about what is out there.

In this chapter we will take two of the most common activities associated with graphics for the Web, and look at how a number of the more popular tools handle them. Specifically, we'll be looking at:

- Optimization of images for the Web
- Image slicing

We will cover these topics with the following applications:

- Adobe Photoshop and ImageReady
- Macromedia Fireworks
- JASC Paint Shop Pro

7

Basic Optimization

Optimization for the Web is sort of a double-edged sword. On one hand, you want to carry the sharpness, color, contrast, clarity, and quality of your original image to the Web. On the other hand, if it results in a file that's rather large, it may take too long to download, and impatient users will surf right past it. And so we find ourselves constantly addressing these opposing goals on a case-by-case basis, trying to maintain as much image quality as possible while cramming it into as small a file as possible.

Sometimes we skip using images altogether and rely on plain text, CSS, and vector images, but that is all covered elsewhere in this book. For now, we're going to look at optimization techniques.

Adobe Photoshop

There are a lot of tools out there that can help us get our images on to the web, but we're going to start with the one that has the most momentum in the industry, Adobe Photoshop.

Adobe Photoshop was initially released as a package aimed at the print world, with uses for photographers wanting to do photo manipulation, and later integrated some web optimization features. With the 5.0 release of Photoshop, Adobe recognized that many web developers didn't need the full power of Photoshop, and so they created a stand-alone pared-down version of Photoshop aimed at web developers called ImageReady. Since then, ImageReady has been folded back into Photoshop as a bundled tool (you can't buy it as a stand-alone anymore).

Photoshop allows users to optimize right from within Photoshop, saving the extra step of launching ImageReady. To do this, simply go to File > Save for Web. The dialog box that comes up presents a pretty robust set of options allowing you to play around with different optimization settings. The following screenshots are from **Photoshop 6.0**. For brevity's sake, I'll leave Adobe ImageReady out, as the process is so similar between the two applications.

As you can see, you have the option of comparing up to three views of the image with different optimization settings, with the fourth being the original image. This image shows the GIF optimization settings:

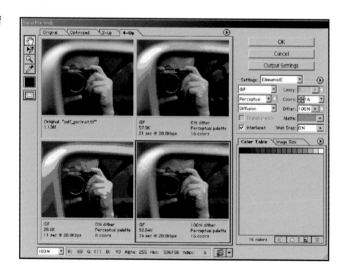

The following image shows the JPEG optimization settings:

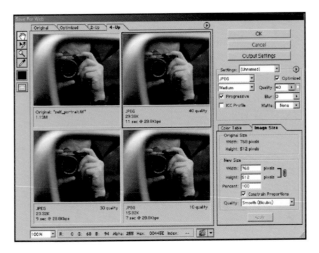

The next image shows PNG optimization settings:

The 4-Up view in Photoshop allows you to quickly view a number of different optimization settings. In these screen captures, you can see that this view allows you to compare the original image, as well as three versions as GIF, JPEG, or PNG. Generally you'll set up four GIFs or four JPEGs or four PNGs side-by-side to compare the different settings, but the previous sample shows a quick comparison available among the three.

We'll explain what the tools do, and what the information in the windows represents. Taking the toolbar first, the hand icon allows you to move the image around in the viewing pane, in case some of it is obscured:

The second tool is a knife; it acts as the slicing tool. Using this tool, you can divide the image up into pieces so Photoshop can output it as sliced images into an HTML template. If you click the bottom-most button, it toggles the display of the slices, so you can see them or ignore them.

The magnifying glass simply lets you zoom in or out, and the eyedropper allows you to select a color, which will appear in place of the black in the button below it. Clicking this button will bring up the color selector dialog box.

Next, the four tabs allow you to view the original, an image of the optimized version, or a two- or four-image comparison:

The arrow to the right allows you to choose a color space (such as Windows or Macintosh), show how a browser might dither your colors, and select a default modem speed for the download time estimates displayed beneath each image.

The text at the top of the following screenshot is associated with each preview image:

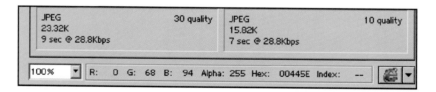

It tells you the basic optimization settings you have chosen for that image, as well as the file size and estimated download time based on the modem speed selected above. This is important to note, as you'll want to ensure your pages don't take too long to download. The images I use in my examples are significantly larger than I would use in a web page, but that is only to show them clearly in this book.

Below that is a select menu that you can use to quickly set the zoom. To the right is a set of numbers showing the RGB color values, alpha transparency, and hex color value of whatever pixel the mouse is hovering over.

The button to the right is a quick browser preview option. You can choose the browser you want, and when you click the button itself, it launches a browser with an optimized version of the image and its basic file information.

The GIF optimization settings allow you to choose the palette (web-safe, adaptive, etc.), the type of dithering (if any) and how much, how many colors you want in your palette, transparency and matte color, and interlacing:

You can also set how much colors snap to their web-safe equivalents, and there is even an option to include "lossy" compression in your GIF file. The little arrow allows you to set a target file size for optimization, as well as save your settings and refresh the views. As we saw in the chapter 6, GIF files only allow for one level of transparency - a pixel is either a color or transparent, but never partially transparent. As such, if we want to use a color that matches the background color of our web page, we use the matte settings and Photoshop and ImageReady will blend a series of pixels to that color to make the transparency a smooth transition to the background color.

Below that is a color palette that mimics the one that Photoshop has used internally for years, making it much easier for experienced users to understand the interface, and for novice users to remember the interface in the main application, in ImageReady, and in these optimization dialogs. You can add colors, modify colors, and delete colors. You can even lock colors so they don't shift as you play with the optimization settings. Locking a color is simply a matter of clicking on the color you wish to lock into place, and pressing the padlock button below. This puts a small white square in the lower right corner of the color that has been locked, and will prevent it from shifting even if you reduce or expand the available colors.

The JPEG output settings allow you to choose the quality of the JPEG - basically it controls the tradeoff between image quality and file size:

The 'progressive' option is akin to interlacing in a GIF - it allows a browser to display the image with more and more detail as it downloads. The Blur setting allows you to eke smaller file sizes out of the image by making it less sharp. If your image has transparency, you can set a matte color (essentially the background color), since JPEG doesn't support transparency. Finally, you can embed an ICC color profile in your image, although this usually results in a much larger image with no real benefit for your users. This color profile is generally reserved for the print world to allow professional print houses to import the color settings you used when creating the images so that the colors will match. As such, you won't find too much use for that feature on the Web, unless the source images you are creating may also go to print.

Beneath these options, we don't need the color table for JPEG compression, so I've switched it to the image-sizing option so we can look at that. Just in case you forgot to resize your image, never fear, you can do a quick resize just as if you were still within Photoshop instead of in the image optimization dialog box.

You'll note the button labeled Output Settings near the top of the optimization dialog (previous screenshot). This option allows you to control the HTML output of the page, if you choose to output HTML along with your image, as well as the filename format, and even some other details of the HTML:

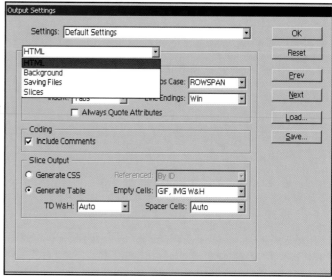

This is very handy for rapid prototyping, but probably isn't such a good idea for final HTML. While the HTML isn't as bad as that from some tools out there, it won't win any awards for compliance or simplicity.

Now let's imagine you've actually gotten through all that and you even want to save the image. Now you have the option to save just the image itself, or an HTML file based on your preferences - uh, oh! Did you forget to set your HTML output preferences on the previous screen? No problem, the same option is here as well, right under the File name:

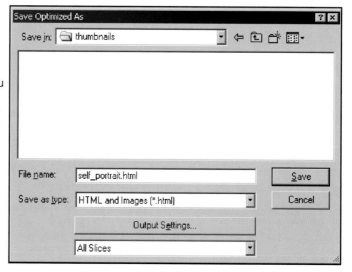

Macromedia Fireworks

Macromedia released Fireworks to fill a bit of a niche. Aimed at the web developer, it offers not only a robust photo-editing set of tools, but also vector-drawing tools, and integrated optimization tools. You won't get all the photo-editing features of Photoshop (especially high-resolution support for print jobs), but if you don't have an illustration package (Macromedia FreeHand, Illustrator, CorelDraw, etc.), this will likely be enough to create vector art for both web and Flash development. These images are from **Fireworks MX**. You can get a free trial of Fireworks for 30 days at the Macromedia web site. It's worth the trial to get a feel for whether or not it's a good fit for the way you work.

There is an Export Wizard that walks you through the process of optimizing an image, but we're just going to skip that here since it's pretty self-explanatory, and if you're reading this it would really be pretty redundant.

You can see similarities to the Photoshop optimization dialog box, the main difference being that the toolbars for the application itself are visible, as these features are always available without having to go into an export mode:

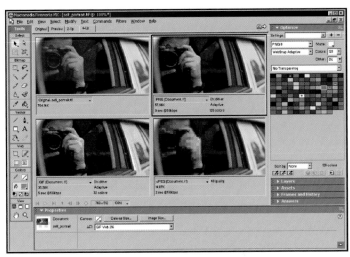

Now that you've seen some of the tools in Photoshop's arsenal, you should recognize their analogs in Fireworks. For the most part, you'll find they work the same way, although there is some room for variation.

Much like Photoshop's optimization dialog, Fireworks also allows you to view your image alongside up to three different views with varying optimization settings:

That button on the end allows you to send your work to other Macromedia products such as FreeHand, Dreamweaver, Flash, or Director by saving the current file in the appropriate format. What's nice about this feature is that it exports only the data native to the target application - Dreamweaver will be sent HTML, Flash and FreeHand will get vector information, and Director will get layers and slices. It also allows you to preview the image in a primary and secondary browser, or just export the HTML. And just to show it plays well with others, it even lets you export to Photoshop, Illustrator, GoLive, and FrontPage. How nice is that?

Also like the Photoshop dialog, Fireworks shows the basic image optimization settings beneath each preview, along with the final file size and estimated download speed:

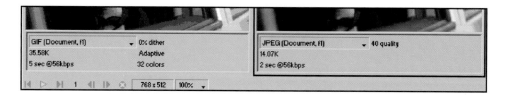

Below that, we can see the animation controls (disabled for this preview), and to the right of them are the pixel dimensions of the image and its current zoom factor (as well as the ability to change that zoom).

For the most part, you'll find the GIF optimization palettes tend to be consistent across applications:

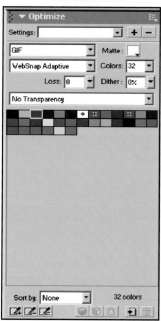

Here you can set the number of colors, choose or load the color palette, set specific colors or an alpha channel to be transparent, add, modify, and remove colors, and even lock colors into place (indicated by a diamond on a white square). Like Photoshop's "lossy" setting, Fireworks has a "loss" setting, allowing you to sacrifice detail for better image compression. You cannot, however, choose the type of dithering pattern you want to use for dithers in your image, just the density of the dither. In order to set your GIF as interlaced, you need to hit that tiny little striped button-thing in the dark stripe across the top, where a number of other useful options are also hidden, although most of them are related to the interface of the tool:

Being able to sort colors, however, is pretty handy, and we can see that on the bottom, right above the three buttons on the left that allow you to add or modify what colors are transparent in your GIF. Sorting allows you to view the colors organized by their luminance, essentially going from brightest to darkest, and it allows you to sort the colors based on how much they are used in the image, making it a bit easier to determine if it's safe to delete a color before you go and do it:

The PNG-8 settings in Fireworks are much like the GIF settings, as you can see in the image:

The PNG-24 and PNG-32 settings are similar to the JPEG options, but without control over the quality or blurriness of the image.

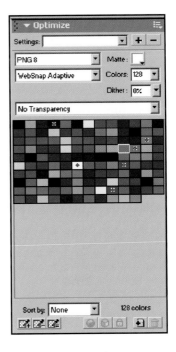

The JPEG options have a nice twist to them that allows you to create some lean images that otherwise might be a little too large for your average site. That purple-ish box over my face is actually a special JPEG mask I created in Fireworks that allows just that area of the image to have a different compression setting than the rest of the image:

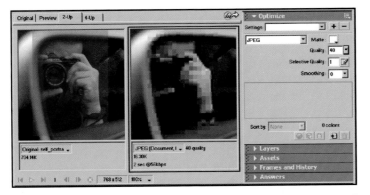

This feature is called "selective quality," and as you can see in the sample, I set my face to have the worst quality compression, while the rest of the image comes in with a much higher quality. This exaggerated example shaved 1.4kb off my sample photograph. Ideally, we'd set the parts of the image that have less detail or that we don't care about (usually the background rather than the subject's face, as I have done) to have a lower compression setting so we can squeeze a smaller file out of the image without sacrificing the quality of the main element within the image. An additional bonus is that you can control the settings: you get a custom overlay color, and you can preserve the quality of text and buttons automatically, saving you the hassle of complex masking for optimization's sake.

JASC Paint Shop Pro

Paint Shop Pro has long existed as an inexpensive alternative to Adobe Photoshop on the Windows platform (one-sixth the price for the full version), and has also recognized the need to integrate image optimization tools into its features. It takes a slightly different approach from the Photoshop and Fireworks model of giant integrated tool palettes. Paint Shop Pro enjoys a good number of loyal users and the Web is littered with tutorial sites. For these examples, we'll be examining **Paint Shop Pro 7**.

So here's another walk-through of basic image optimization, this time in Paint Shop Pro. You'll immediately note that it isn't quite the same as doing it in Photoshop or Fireworks. The process is a bit more clunky, and it's not as integrated into the interface, but it still works well.

In order to access the optimization tools in Paint Shop Pro, you need to look under File > Export. From there you can choose between the JPEG, GIF, or PNG Optimizer:

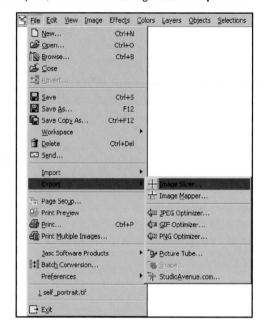

The three output options (GIF, JPEG, PNG) use very similar dialog boxes. This first is for GIF, and we immediately see that we can't preview more than one setting at a time, and the options are spread across 5 tabs:

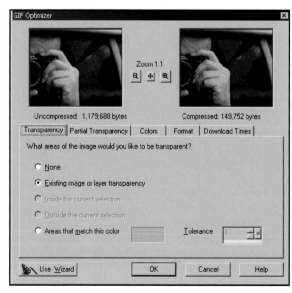

The transparency setting doesn't allow you to select a color directly from the preview; you have to move the dialog out of the way and select a color from the original image beneath. You can still use an alpha channel or a selection to choose what parts of an image may be transparent, and you can also insert the value for any color. You have the ability to control how much variance in that color will be tolerated and still count the color as transparent, something that is useful for images without flat color.

Between the photos are a pair of magnifying glasses that allow the user to zoom in or out, as well as a four-way arrow that briefly pops up a small view of the overall image and a box outlining the thumbnail to make it easier to position what parts of the image the two thumbnails display.

The Partial Transparency tab gives the novice user some valuable information on how transparency works, by noting that pixels in GIF images can't be partially transparent and prompting the user to make some decisions about what happens to pixels that are partially transparent in the source image:

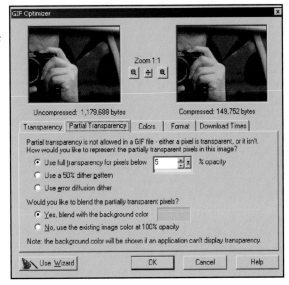

Here, on the Colors tab, the user can select the size of the color palette, the amount of dithering (although not the style), and can choose from some pre-built palettes:

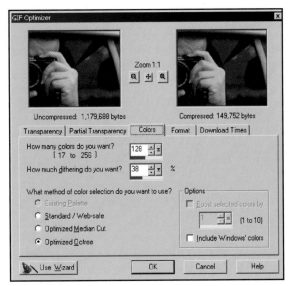

The user cannot select a new palette, adjust colors, lock any colors, or otherwise massage the palette. These actions can be performed before going to export, so it's a matter of the order you do things in.

On the Format tab, the user can select between an interlaced and non-interlaced GIF:

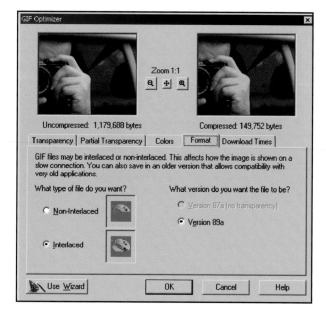

For the novice, the animated icons showing how the two images would load on a web page is a good way to help make the decision easier.

The JPEG optimization dialog looks similar to the GIF dialog, but with fewer tabs and fewer options. For instance, you cannot choose a color palette, JPEG doesn't support transparency, and instead of being interlaced a JPEG would be progressive. Here the user can select the quality of the JPEG:

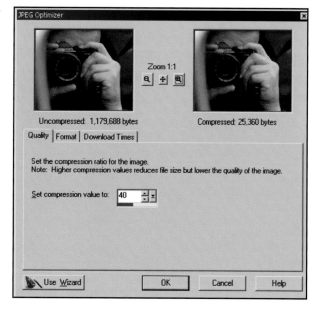

Just as we saw in the GIF dialog box, the user can select between progressive and standard JPEGs, with similar icons and explanation:

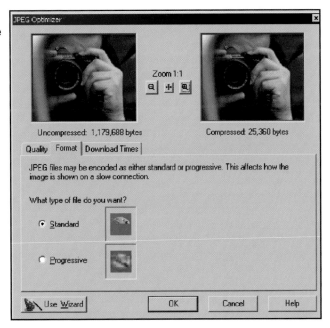

This last tab, Download Times, exists in GIF, JPEG, and PNG dialogs, and simply offers the user a guide to the size of the file, as well as a rough guide to download times at different connection speeds:

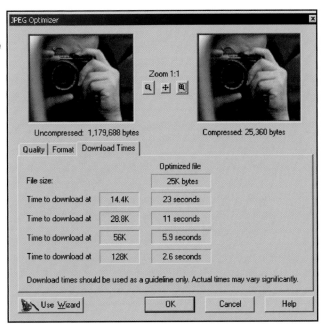

The PNG dialog handles both PNG-8 and PNG-24 images, although all the options on this dialog go away if you choose PNG-24 (such as color control, the optimization options, and transparency options). Otherwise, this tab is designed for the PNG-8 format and functions pretty much like the GIF dialog:

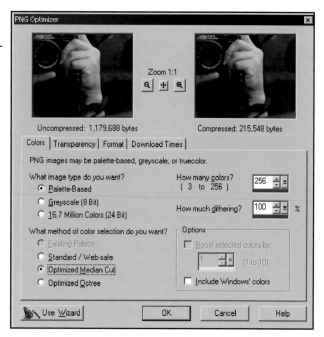

The PNG Transparency options also function like the GIF transparency options, but for both PNG-8 and PNG-24:

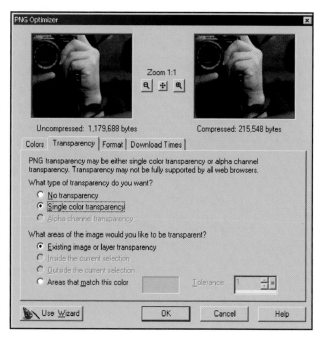

If you've used the interlaced or progressive options from GIF or JPEG, respectively, then the dialog on the Format tab here is familiar:

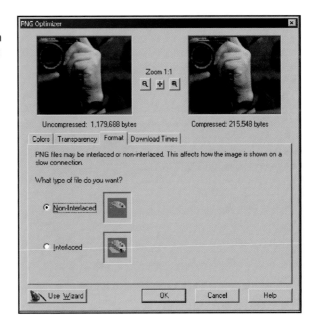

Image Slicing

Each of the image packages we've looked at so far also does something called image slicing. This is particularly handy if you have a large image you'd like to break up into pieces in order to achieve better optimization for different sections, or even for those rare instances where the entire page is an image. It can even be useful for quick prototypes to show clients or just get a feel for how a design may look in the browser. In practice, pages that consist of nothing but sliced images aren't going to be terribly accessible or usable for your users. However there are cases where the page is about the design, and that is the content, so please consider this when using the image slicing feature of these packages.

If, however, you find yourself creating an entire site with images, including the copy, you might want to take a moment to jump back to the typography chapter and look through the caveats associated with setting your text content in images. It's also too easy to create bloated pages since none of these applications will automatically reuse images, other than spacers in areas of flat color. And don't forget, there is no such thing as pixel-precise layouts when dealing with the vagaries of browsers, screen settings, browser text settings, and all sorts of other factors. Sometimes a space in the code is enough to blow up a layout. Relying less on sliced layouts and more on hand-tweaked layouts designed to look good regardless of precise control over how the user sees it, will guarantee a longer shelf life and generally be more usable to your visitors.

As before, we'll look at each of the main three packages and how they deal with image slicing.

ImageReady

We walked through Photoshop for the image optimization instead of ImageReady, because the two are so similar in their optimization settings. Photoshop, however, does not have any slicing capability, and so we use its sister application, ImageReady, in this case **ImageReady 3** (version 3 comes with Photoshop 7).

In ImageReady, you can create slices in a number of ways, but my favorite is to use pre-existing page guides that you may already have set up (either in Photoshop or ImageReady) when you were designing your image and aligning the various elements. Either way, you can always combine slices, split them, draw new ones, and otherwise tweak them to get just what you're looking for. As we can see from the following screenshot, not only have we split the photo up into six even blocks, we've set different optimization settings for each in order to show some sample output:

The palettes we can see include the tool palette that allows us to manipulate the slice edges themselves, as well as a familiar-looking optimization palette. Above the document, we can see some tools that allow us to align the slices with one another, as well as to shift their location around. Below we can see the palette that allows us to choose the image name for each slice (with the default text left in place for now), and set a background color for the table cell that will hold the image. We can even make the image into a link by providing a URL. This is all because ImageReady will even output the HTML for us, with some stylistic preferences from us (tag case, for example). Of course, those of us who are HTML purists will still want to go in and tweak the code, since it's still too easy to output overly complex or verbose code, and depending on your settings, invalid code as well.

Opposite we can see the page in the browser after we've output the HTML and all the images:

Fireworks

Just as with the optimization controls, experience in ImageReady will give you a leg up when wading through the options for Fireworks. Even if you haven't used ImageReady, much of what we've covered above is applicable to Fireworks. Fireworks offers you the same ability to slice the image, and the same freedom to rework those slices into precisely the size you want.

Fireworks has a unique feature, however, that allows you to create non-rectangular slices. This is very useful for when you are creating an image rollover and you don't want the entire image to roll over. It doesn't create a non-rectangular image; it simply ensures you don't swap background elements when using rollovers on things like image maps.

And of course, you have all the regular elements of a slice you can control, including optimization settings, links, and even alt attributes for the images. Just like ImageReady, Fireworks will output the HTML for you as well. Again, you may wish to wade into the code and change it up to match your personal style and make sure it's as clean as you can get it:

Opposite is the final output as seen in the browser:

Paint Shop Pro

As with our optimization walk-through, Paint Shop Pro breaks from the interfaces common to ImageReady and Fireworks. Just as the optimization tools aren't integrated directly into the interface, we have to go to the same menu to find the slicing tools, File > Image Slicer. This launches a dialog that cannot be resized and all-too-often does not show enough of what you need to see. It also doesn't have the optimization controls built into the dialog. Instead, you have to open up the same optimization dialog we used before for each slice:

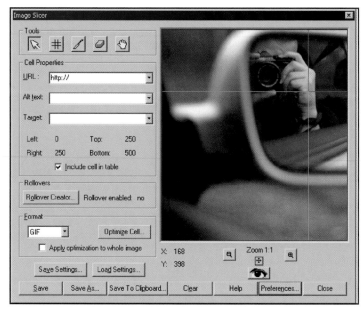

As you can see, you can set alt text for the images, as well as URLs so they can become hyperlinks. You also have the option to launch the rollover dialog, as well as the optimization dialog. The eye icon allows you to preview your work in a web browser. Again, the resulting browser output is shown below:

Other Image Utilities

There are many other image editing utilities out there that are either geared specifically to the Web, or have had web-export features built in. To go into detail on all of them here would quickly take over this book, but I will list some alternatives out there for you to explore on your own.

If these don't fit your needs, a few minutes searching popular download sites and graphics forums will usually point you in the right direction. No matter what your platform or budget, there's almost always something available that can fit.

Photoshop Forums:
http://www.listmoms.net/lists/photoshop/
http://www.adobe.com/support/forums/

Fireworks Forums:
http://groups.yahoo.com/group/Fireworks/
http://webforums.macromedia.com/fireworks/

Paint Shop Pro:
http://groups.yahoo.com/group/paintshoppro/

Graphics Café:
http://www.listmoms.net/lists/graphics-cafe/

evolt.org Mailing List:
http://evolt.org/

Babble Mailing List:
http://www.babblelist.com/

WebDesign-L Mailing List:
http://www.webdesign-l.com/

Corel Photo-Paint

One of the originals on the scene, Photo-Paint is often used as an alternative to Adobe Photoshop, especially by Windows users. Over the years, as Corel has grown it with the rest of its graphics suite, it has also been expanded with support for GIF and JPEG optimization. You can find out more about Photo-Paint at the Corel site: *http://www.corel.com/.*

The GIMP

Don't worry; this isn't something sleeping in the box in Zed's basement. The GIMP (GNU Image Manipulation Program) is a freeware image-editing package that runs on Unix and X, a platform generally ignored by the more familiar makers in the graphics world. There is also a version for Microsoft Windows, although the installation process is not exactly as simple as installing Photoshop or Fireworks.

You can find out more, see screen captures, and download the most recent version at the GIMP web site at *http://www.gimp.org/*. It features not only the download of the application, but also tutorials, documentation, support groups, news, and other information.

Macromedia Flash

Given that we have a chapter in this book detailing vector animation and Flash, I won't repeat the same information again except to say that it is possible to consider a Flash movie just the same way you might consider a GIF, JPEG, or PNG on a page. You don't need to restrict Flash to creating entire multimedia sites. Sometimes Flash is perfect for creating a logo or other unique image that integrates a little motion, interactivity, or even audio. If it's not integral to making the site function, then you needn't worry about the issues of accessibility for the most part.

Summary

We've gone over a sampling of the features available in Fireworks, Photoshop/ImageReady, and Paint Shop Pro. Keep in mind that this is not a comprehensive tutorial; this is just an overview of the more common features. Each of these packages offers full tutorials for nearly all of its features, as well as extensive online support.

8

- Macromedia Flash

- Scalable Vector Graphics

- Synchronized Multimedia Integration Language

- Issues when dealing with vector graphics on the web

Author: Nick Boyce

Vector Graphics for the Web

In this chapter we shall be introducing and discussing vector graphics. It's not going to be an exhaustive discussion, but we'll give you enough information to make an informed decision about where, when and how to use vector graphics.

As an alternative to the bitmap graphic formats we looked at in *Chapter 7*, vector graphics have a number of differences that need to be understood before they can be used effectively. Specifically, we'll be looking at the most widespread format, **Macromedia Flash**, as well as two formats for which support is increasing, **SVG** (Scalable Vector Graphics) and **SMIL** (Synchronized Multimedia Integration Language). We'll start with an explanation of what vector graphics are, where they come from, why you would want to use them, and when you wouldn't. We'll also take some examples of what you can do with vector graphics, from basic shapes to simple animation.

Interactivity is a big part of what the formats we are looking at can offer, and we will look into some of what they can offer through their respective scripting languages. We'll also discuss the advantages and disadvantages of using these different formats.

A Quick History

Before the advent of the World Wide Web, the Internet was restricted to plain text and any associated images had to be distributed through other methods such as E-mail, Usenet, Telnet, et al. When the World Wide Web and its markup language HTML came onto the scene, the power to combine text with GIF and JPEG images sparked a massive surge of interest in the Web.

8

It wasn't long before demand grew for multimedia - the combining of text, graphics, video, and audio - to create an entirely new user experience and new possibilities for communication. This spawned numerous creative attempts to "push the envelope" of multimedia possibilities through browser add-ons called "plugins". While many were stillborn or quickly fizzled out, the most famous and web-altering success stories are Macromedia's Flash (for vector graphics and animation) and RealAudio (for streaming audio and video).

It wasn't long before Flash became the de facto standard for online vector graphics and animation, and it remains the most widely installed plugin available. Flash - in its latest release as Flash MX - is a mature product, which incorporates not only animation and vector graphics, but also support for video, interactivity including form elements, and complex server communication and scripting features.

In 1999 a group of industry leaders (including Adobe, Apple, Macromedia, Microsoft, Netscape, and Sun) formed the SVG Working Group to create an open-standard vector graphic format, combining the best features of Vector Markup Language (VML) and Precision Graphics Markup Language (PGML). The resulting format is SVG (Scaleable Vector Graphics), which is the WC3 (World Wide Web Consortium) standard for delivery of online vector graphics.

The SVG format renders vector graphics in the browser using plain text markup based on XML and is causing a great deal of excitement. While the format is still a long way behind gaining the sort of widespread adoption Flash enjoys, significant industry support - such as Adobe's SVG viewer being installed standard with Acrobat Reader - and an increasing range of authoring and viewing software, should see the use of SVG increase significantly in the future.

As vector graphics on the Web have evolved, they are used for so much more than just graphics - SVG and Flash can both handle rich animation and interactivity which represent an exciting future for the Web.

We'll discuss both of these formats later in this chapter, as well as briefly look at another W3C format: SMIL (Synchronized Multimedia Integration Language). SMIL (pronounced "smile") aims to assemble and synchronize different media to create multimedia presentations.

Principles

One of the main advantages of using vector graphics online is that the file sizes can be significantly smaller than their bitmap equivalents, and they can scale seamlessly and infinitely. To understand the differences between vector graphics and bitmap graphics, let's have a look at how they work.

Bitmap graphics such as JPEG and GIF files are based on a grid of dots on the screen, called pixels. Each pixel of a bitmap image contains color information, so naturally the more pixels that make up the image, the bigger the file size.

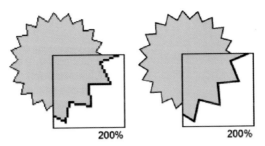

200%   200%

The vector image on the right is created from mathematical information that defines the path and the color of the fill. Because screens are pixel-based, vector graphics are transformed from mathematical formulae into pixels by the computer's CPU and graphics card at display time. This means that the vectors can be scaled to any size, but it also means that a heavy load is placed on the CPU and graphics card to display complex vector shapes - especially when it comes to animations where the CPU must continually render vector information into pixels for display.

As the detail of the diagrams show, bitmapped images will distort and "pixelate" if scaled to any larger than 100% of their original size. This is because bitmaps have a fixed number of pixels that make up the image; if you increase the size of the image, you are simply increasing the size of the pixels.

While vector graphics are great for logos and other images involving relatively large, contiguous blocks of colors, JPEG and PNG still reign supreme for creationing photographic imagery, which is typically composed of small, scattered, and highly varying clusters of colors. A vector graphic can be transformed into a bitmap - but it can be complicated and inefficient to transform a bitmap into a vector graphic. Vector graphics rely on shapes and simple fills, rather than individual pixels, so creating a photographic image in vector is impractical. The vector formats we will look at in this chapter can import or embed images, so there is no need to transform bitmap images into vectors to use them on the Web.

Vector Graphic Formats

As we've mentioned, there are a number of formats available for creating and displaying vector graphics in the web browser, the most readily available being Flash. As we'll see, there are other formats available, and we'll be looking at SVG (Scalable Vector Graphics), and SMIL (Synchronized Multimedia Integration Language). For each format we'll look at how easy it is to create basic shapes and simple animation, as well as some examples of how each technology has been used effectively on the Internet. We'll also provide you with some useful links, in case you wish to expand your knowledge of these formats.

Macromedia Flash

Some see the Flash as the "eye candy" of the Internet, and certainly in the early years, its primary use was as a tool for delivery of animation and vector graphics. Although Flash has enjoyed success in animating anything from games through product demonstrations to music clips, Macromedia has changed its focus, moving Flash into the area of delivering client-side. In this chapter we are going to focus on Flash's graphics and animation capabilities, though we will discuss some of the principles of Flash's advanced features. Designers can use Flash to complement an HTML layout, or design a page that has no visual HTML elements at all and use Flash as the main focus.

Flash is the name for the file format (SWF or Shockwave Flash) as well as the primary tool for authoring Flash content: Macromedia Flash. Flash MX, the latest version of this authoring software coincided with the release of the latest Flash plugin: Flash Player 6.

Macromedia has some key partnerships that see the plugin installed on most Windows and Macintosh computers, as well as the latest versions of Internet Explorer, Netscape, AOL, and Web TV clients. Macromedia claim Flash content can be viewed by more than 90% of Internet browsers, with the latest player, Flash 6, having around 30% penetration.

Although the format is proprietary and controlled by Macromedia, this has its advantages. The major advantage is that the Flash player that Macromedia distributes controls delivery of all Flash content, meaning that playback is consistent across all browsers and devices where it is installed.

The Flash Workspace

When Macromedia opened the Flash File Format (SWF) sourcecode in 1999, it meant that any developer who follows the licensing agreement is able to create software that will play or author the Flash format. This has lead to some interesting uses for the Flash format (such as a Flash rendering engine built for Playstation 2 software), and there are now many great tools and utilities for Flash authoring besides Macromedia's Flash.

The most comprehensive Flash authoring package besides Macromedia's own is Adobe LiveMotion, which uses a timeline style based on their video compositing tool After Effects. Trial versions of both Flash and LiveMotion are available from Macromedia and Adobe's web sites respectively. There have also been a number of software packages developed for creating animations (Swish), screensavers (Screentime) as well as utilities for vector path compression (Optimaze) and 3D software integration (Swift). For information on these products, take a look at the following web sites:

- **Macromedia Flash Tryout**: *http://www.macromedia.com/software/trial_download/*
- **Adobe LiveMotion Tryout**: *http://www.adobe.com/products/tryadobe/main.jhtml*
- Flash authoring tool **Swish**: *http://www.swishzone.com*
- **Screentime**: *http://www.screentime.com/*
- **Optimaze**: *http://www.file-size.com/flash/index.html*
- Vector 3D tool **Swift**: *http://www.erain.com*
- More Flash software and utilities: *http://www.actionscript.org/software/*

Given that most Flash content is authored in Macromedia's Flash, let's have a look at the workspace in the latest version - Flash MX:

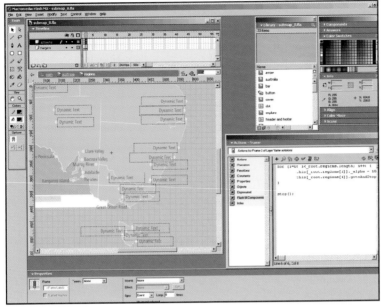

The Flash workspace provides everything a developer needs to create a Flash file from start to finish. Some designers choose to create all of their vector graphics in Flash, while others prefer to design in other software like Macromedia FreeHand, Corel DRAW or Adobe Illustrator and import the final artwork. Bitmap images can be imported into Flash movies but not edited, so in order to edit a bitmap an external editor such as Photoshop must be used.

Let's take a look at the areas of the Flash MX workspace.

Toolbox

The toolbox contains tools for selecting, editing, and creating objects as well as zooming and adjusting the view of the stage.

Timeline and Layers

Each part of the grid in the timeline represents a frame, which controls a movie's content over time. The layers help organize the movie's content.

Library

The library organizes the movie's symbols - Movie Clips, Buttons, Graphics, and Bitmaps.

Stage

The stage is where graphics are created and edited.

Actions

The Actions palette is where Flash's scripts - called ActionScripts - are written and edited.

Panels

Flash has a collection of panels, which make it possible to edit properties of almost any object in the movie.

Property Inspector

The properties inspector is a contextual toolbar that displays frequently used settings for a tool or object.

ActionScript

Although Flash is a visual environment, the real power of Flash is realized through controlling it with ActionScript.

ActionScript is the object-oriented programming language at the core of Flash, which can control just about anything within a Flash movie. ActionScript in Flash 5 was revised from the ground up to be compliant with the ECMAScript standard, meaning that syntax, object model, and some classes are nearly identical to JavaScript.

Despite their similarities, there are some important differences between JavaScript and ActionScript. JavaScript operates in the browser, which means it has access to the browser's DOM (Document Object Model) whereas ActionScript can only call objects contained in Flash movies. Although it is possible to make ActionScript communicate with external Javascripts, this functionality is not available on all browsers and platforms.

Flash authoring software such as Macromedia's Flash and Adobe's LiveMotion both feature tools to add ActionScripts to Flash. We'll look at some basic ActionScript later in this chapter, but before we can understand ActionScript, we must understand the way that Flash treats its objects.

The Flash Object Model

Flash uses an internal object model in much the same way as JavaScript uses the browser's DOM. The Flash object model consists of movie clips, text fields, and buttons. It is important to understand the way that the Flash object model works, as it is a critical part of working with Flash, particularly when using ActionScript.

The most common objects for Flash to interact with are "movie clips". Not to be confused with SWF movies (the final compiled movie that Flash outputs), Flash's movie clips are objects that contain their own timelines and can be used multiple times within a Flash document.

Every movie clip in a Flash file is contained within Flash's Library, and when it is added to the stage it creates an "instance" of that movie clip. There can be many instances of each movie clip on the stage, and they can all be treated independently of each other.

Movie clips can also be "nested" inside each other. For example, a picture of a face might be made up of eyes, mouth, nose, ears, and hair. The eyes object could have nested movie clips inside it for eyelids and eye color. These nested - or "child" - objects can be controlled independently or "inherit" properties from the "parent" object. It also means that animation timelines can be controlled independently in nested movie clips.

Being an "object-oriented" programming language, ActionScript programming is about controlling the properties of these instances.

Using the Flash Object Model

The following example is an interactive map of Australia, which uses nested movie clips for the different levels of interactivity within the movie. The map has been imported from Macromedia FreeHand, and I have used the Optimize Curves tool to reduce the complexity of the shape within Flash MX. The rest of the artwork has been created directly within Flash.

The figure shows an instance of the map of Australia called "map" on the main timeline of the movie. In order to create rollovers to highlight each state, I have attached behaviors to buttons and placed the buttons over the states.

The following code has been attached to the button that represents New South Wales and Australian Capital Territory by selecting the button and adding the following code to the Actions window.

```
on (rollOver) {
    map.gotoAndStop("nsw");
}


on (rollOut) {
    map.gotoAndStop("off");
}

on (press) {

    gotoAndPlay("state7");
}
```

Those familiar with JavaScript will recognize the syntax immediately. This code uses the `rollover` event handler to tell the movie clip instance "map" to go to a marker in its timeline called "nsw". At that location is a highlighted version of the New South Wales region. Because this frame is located within the "map" movie clip, it can be controlled independently of the main timeline, as shown below:

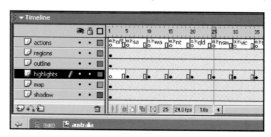

Inside the "map" movie clip is another clip called "regions", which contains text fields and circles to represent and label regions on the map. These text fields are populated from live information contained within a database using the `loadVariables` command. We won't get into client / server communication here as we will discuss it later in the chapter.

The result - seen at *www.australianholidaycentre.com.au* - is a zoomable map which allows for quick navigation through a database of travel packages. Because the map is made up of vector information rather than pixels, the scaling is smooth and there is no distortion.

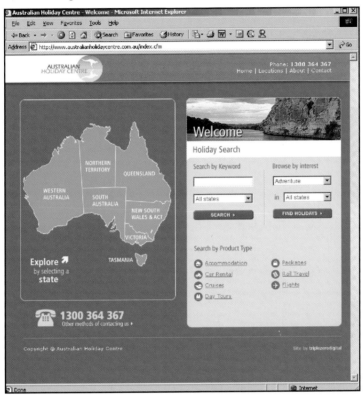

At the Australian Holiday Center site, Flash is used to complement rather than replace HTML pages, and an alternative version is provided (in the form of a GIF with an image map) for users without the Flash plugin.

Loading on Demand

Within Flash movies it is possible to create instances of internal movie clips, but also possible to load multiple external SWF movies into the Flash Player on demand, without directing the web browser to a different URL. This makes it possible to load information into the browser as needed, rather than waiting for one larger movie to download.

What's more, separating the data gives the developer complete control over what happens during the loading process. They may want to show a game if the loading will take some time (simple games in Flash can be entertaining and only use several kilobytes) and display some key points about the section they are going to, or a loading progress bar.

When content is loading seamlessly into Flash movies, critical content like text can be loaded first, leaving sounds and images to download as the user reads the text. Flash MX has also introduced functionality to load JPEG images and MP3 audio files directly into the Flash Player without having to place them in SWF files.

The `loadMovie` ActionScript function is used to load a SWF file into a movie clip instance - where it adopts the clip's properties such as scale and rotation. Let's have a look at the code for loading external SWF files into the Flash movies.

```
movieClip.loadMovie("moviename.swf")
```

The `movieClip` parameter tells Flash which movie clip instance to load the movie into. The `moviename` in the brackets refers to the path of the movie you want to load. Flash does not allow for the loading of movies from external servers, so all SWF files loaded into your Flash movie need to be on the same server from which they are called.

Now let's take a look at an example of how separating Flash can be used to load content effectively on demand.

Example - Nike Women

The Australian Nike Women site *(http://nikewomen.com.au)* is an excellent example of loading separate SWF files into the Flash player in order to deliver rich content with minimal loading times. The site uses a combination of vector and bitmap graphics, and most of the loading time is taken up by loading the SWF files that use multiple bitmap images.

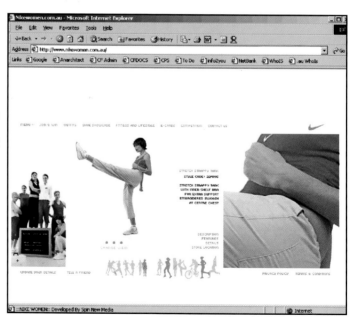

The different elements of the movie are broken up and saved as separate files, and loaded into a "shell" movie, which is only 1Kb in size. The shell movie's job is to be a "container" for the external SWF movies, and load them in using the `loadMovie` command.

Animation

Animation has always been Flash's strong point, and as we mentioned at the start of the chapter, Flash has enjoyed unparalleled success in the delivery of vector-based animations online. Animations can be anything from a splash page to a product demonstration or illustration for a news article.

The animations that Flash creates are frame-based, which means that the animation will play as fast as the frame rate is set when the movie is authored or as fast as the client can render it. Although 12 FPS (frames per second) is the default setting on Flash MX, I usually set my movies to a speed of 24 FPS, which incidentally is the speed at which cinema film is projected. But remember that, high frame rates may cause problems for machines with less CPU power.

Let's have a look at the three main ways to develop animations in Flash.

Frame-by-Frame Animation

Frame-by-frame animation involves creating different images and playing them sequentially - much like how the individual frames of a cartoon appear to move when played in order. This mode of animation is commonly used for splash pages and - of course - cartoons, and is a linear animation style meaning that it is not easily controlled by interactivity. It can also increase file sizes dramatically, so it is not really recommended.

Keyframe Animation

Keyframe animation - also known as "tweening" - is the easiest and most common way to create animations in Flash. The word "tweening" is a traditional cell animation term to describe where a lead artist would create the keyframes (frames which represent major changes in the animation), and an assistant would draw the "in between" frames.

Flash uses these principles of creating seamless transitions between keyframes on the timeline. Flash can animate the size, color, shape, position, opacity, and just about any property of an object using keyframes.

Creating Keyframe Animations

In this 10-frame sequence, we will place an instance of a movie clip - in this case a square - onto the stage and animate its size and rotation over time.

We use the rectangle drawing tool to create the square at a size of 100 by 100 pixels. By selecting this object and choosing *Insert > Convert to Symbol*, we are able to make the square a graphic or movie clip that is added to Flash's library and can now be animated. Flash can only animate graphic symbols and movie clips that are contained in the library. If you try to animate anything other than a symbol, Flash will turn it into a symbol and put it into the library for you.

By selecting the 10th frame in the timeline and choosing *Insert > Keyframe* we can create a keyframe on frame 10 of the timeline. There are many ways to transform a graphic in Flash, but in this case we are going to use the Transform palette (it can be accessed by going to *Window > Transform*) to enter precise measurements of 200% scale and 100 degrees of rotation.

In the resulting animation, Flash does the hard work and creates the 8 variations between the keyframes on frames 1 and 10. We can see the results by either pressing the enter key or selecting *Control > Test Movie*.

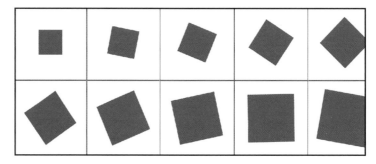

If we add a keyframe in the middle of the sequence, Flash will create the transition between all three points. In this example, I have added a keyframe on frame 6 and given the instance a color tint using the color tint option in the Property Inspector.

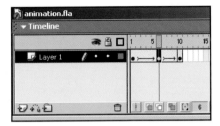

The timeline is changed to reflect the third keyframe.

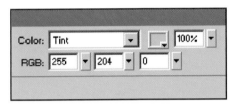

The tint is applied to the shape in the middle keyframe

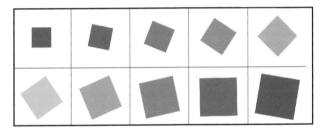

Now the square not only rotates and scales, but transforms its color over time as well. Note that the first and last frames of the sequence are identical to the prior example.

ActionScript-Controlled Animation

Script-based animations are created by manipulating instances of objects with ActionScript. Using ActionScript as an animation tool it is possible to create reactive interfaces, games, and applications that are simply not possible using only keyframe or frame-by-frame animations.

Creating Animations in ActionScript

It is possible to achieve the same results as we achieved in the keyframe animation example by using ActionScript to manipulate the instance's properties. To do this, create the square and turn it into a movie clip as before, then select the instance on the stage and add the following to the Actions palette (you may have to change the palette to Expert mode by clicking on the diagonal arrow to the right of the palette):

```
onClipEvent (enterFrame) {
        this._xscale += 10;
        this._yscale += 10;
        this._rotation += 10;
}
```

The script tells Flash to increase the rotation and scale (on both the x and y axis) of the movie clip by 10 using the `enterFrame` event handler. Using the `enterFrame` handler allows us to perform actions at the same frame rate the Flash movie is set to. Even though the movie is only one frame long, the ActionScript will control the animation regardless of the number of frames.

Of course unless we tell it otherwise, it will animate indefinitely, so if we want to stop it we have to add a condition to the code block like so:

```
onClipEvent (load) {
        var i = 1;
}

onClipEvent (enterFrame) {
        if (i <= 10) {
                this._xscale += 10;
                this._yscale += 10;
                this._rotation += 10;
                i += 1;
        }
}
```

This adds the variable I when the clip loads, using the load event handler. The load event handler is only run when the clip is first loaded and is good for defining variables that are changed though other ActionScripts. We have also added a condition that tells Flash to repeat the `enterFrame` actions only if i is less than 10. At the end of each loop the variable i is increased by 1.

Flash movies with ActionScripts cannot be played inside the Flash timeline so we must use *Control > Test Movie* to view the results.

Keyframe- and ActionScript- controlled animations both have their advantages, but it is a general rule that keyframes are ideal for anything that is linear and ActionScript should be used for dynamic animations. Creating the animation using either ActionScript or keyframe methods has resulted in SWF files that are similar in size: 303 and 283 bytes respectively.

Let's have a look at an example of how ActionScript-controlled animations have made it possible to create an entirely different way of presenting information.

Example - Classic Motown

The Classic Motown web site (*http://www.motown.com/classicmotown*) represents the key points in Motown history from 1959 to 1988. The site takes advantage of ActionScript to create an interface that is both intuitive and engaging.

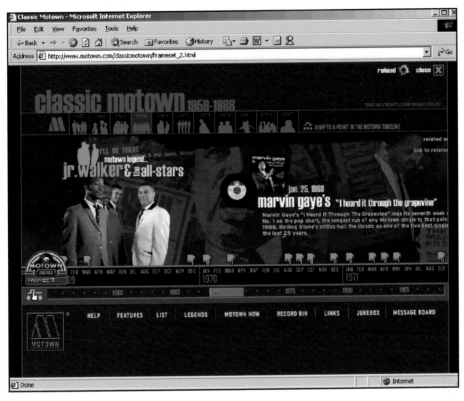

This site makes heavy use of the loadmovie command, loading some 30 movies into the main shell to assemble the main interface. These are loaded sequentially, so that the user always has something to explore when the movies are being loaded.

The main timeline can be browsed either by using the scrollbar to scroll horizontally at the bottom of the screen, or clicking one of the buttons at the top to jump to a particular point. The icons at the top of the page represent key "eras" in the timeline, and by selecting one of these, the timeline jumps to that point.

Fonts

Flash has many and varied uses for text. The most common use is static text, but Flash also has the capability to create dynamic text fields in which values can be changed, and input text, which allows users to enter text in the same way as they would in HTML form.

When you use a font in a Flash movie, Flash embeds the font information in the SWF file, ensuring that the font is displayed properly in the Flash Player. This allows for any typeface the author specifies to be viewed within the resulting SWF file, regardless of whether the viewer has that font installed.

By embedding whole typeface sets, Flash adds around 10-20Kb to the size of the final movie, so it is important not to embed too many fonts into your movie. Using the character option in the properties palette for a textbox, you can limit the amount of the font imported, for example, to only capitals or only the characters you need, which can significantly reduce the download size.

Client/Server Communication

Macromedia has given Flash a powerful toolset for communicating with external data sources, and extensive support for XML, making Flash Player a gateway to access data from varied sources.

Let's take a look at a creative use of Flash's server communication toolset.

Example - They Rule

They Rule (*http://www.theyrule.net*) is a web application, which allows the user to explore the relationships between major corporations and their board members. The site makes use of only a few icon-style graphics, which are duplicated as movie clips for all of the boardroom tables and board members.

Each boardroom table is a "node" that can be expanded and moved to explore the relationships that link them all together. There are also options to perform searches, load and save maps, link to the corporation's web sites and remove nodes from the stage.

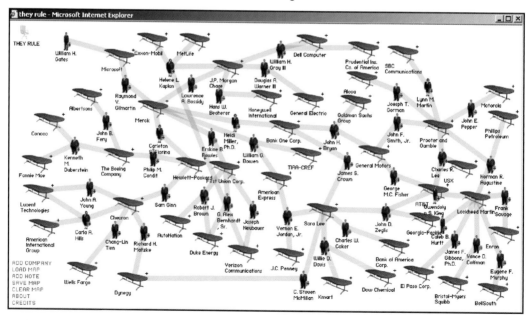

This sort of visualization is a clever use of Flash technology to illustrate a complex set of relationships. The application is essentially a visualization of a complex relational database, imported through the `loadVariables` function in Flash. The data is drawn from a database read by PHP and output in such a way that Flash can understand.

`LoadVariables` is one of the methods of importing data (from a text file or text generated by server-side scripting language such as PHP, ASP, or ColdFusion) into Flash to read or update values in a Flash movie. Flash also has significant support for importing and manipulating XML data.

Data can be sent via GET or POST methods to external sources such as server-side scripts for processing by using the `loadVariables` command, or Flash MX's new `LoadVars` object.

Implementing Flash Content

Flash movies (SWF files) are binary files that are embedded in web pages, much like GIF and JPEG images. Although browsers with the Flash plugin can view .SWF files directly in a browser window, Flash movies are generally referenced by using the `<embed>` and `<object>` tags within a HTML document.

The following code demonstrates how to embed Flash movies into HTML pages. Flash can automatically generate this code for you if you use the Publish command.

```
<!DOCTYPE HTML PUBLIC "-//W3C//DTD HTML 4.0 Transitional//EN">
<HTML>
<HEAD>
<TITLE>A Simple Square</TITLE>
</HEAD>
<BODY bgcolor="#FFFFFF">
<OBJECT classid="clsid:D27CDB6E-AE6D-11cf-96B8-444553540000"
codebase=http://download.macromedia.com/pub/shockwave/cabs/flash/swflash.ca
b#version=6,0,0,0 WIDTH="300" HEIGHT="300" id="square" ALIGN="">
<PARAM NAME=movie VALUE="square.swf">
<PARAM NAME=quality VALUE=high>
<PARAM NAME=bgcolor VALUE=#FFFFFF>
<EMBED src="square.swf" quality=high bgcolor=#FFFFFF WIDTH="300"
HEIGHT="300" NAME="square" ALIGN="" TYPE="application/x-shockwave-flash"
PLUGINSPAGE="http://www.macromedia.com/go/getflashplayer"></EMBED>
</OBJECT>
</BODY>
</HTML>
```

Flash makes use of both the `<object>` and `<embed>` tags. The `<object>` tag is used for Internet Explorer on Windows, and the `<embed>` tag is used for Netscape as well as Internet Explorer on Macintosh.

Let's take a look at two uses of Flash: one that is complementary to HTML and one that seeks to display all information within a Flash movie.

Media Makeup Academy

The Media Makeup Academy (*http://www.mediamakeup.com.au*) web site uses Flash content to complement the content that is produced in HTML and CSS. Flash plays a supporting role to the web site, the top menu and side image are created in Flash to provide extra interactivity, but JPEG files are displayed if a plugin is not detected. We will discuss the importance of plugin detection at the end of this chapter.

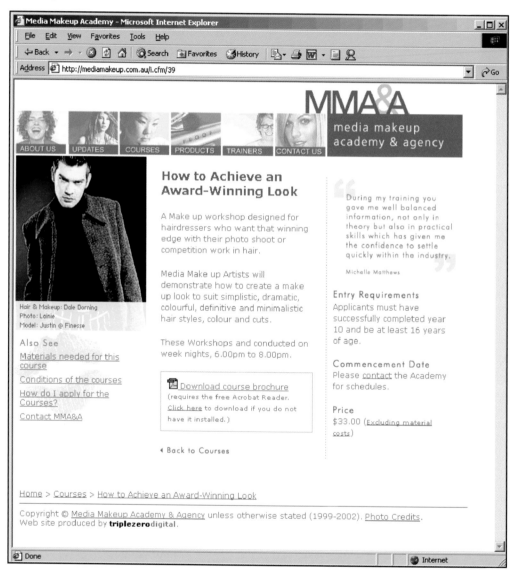

2advanced

2advanced (*http://www.2advanced.com*) have created their whole corporate web site using Flash to load XML and image data on demand. HTML serves as a container for this information, and aside from referencing the Flash file it only contains the most basic visual elements such as a background color and image.

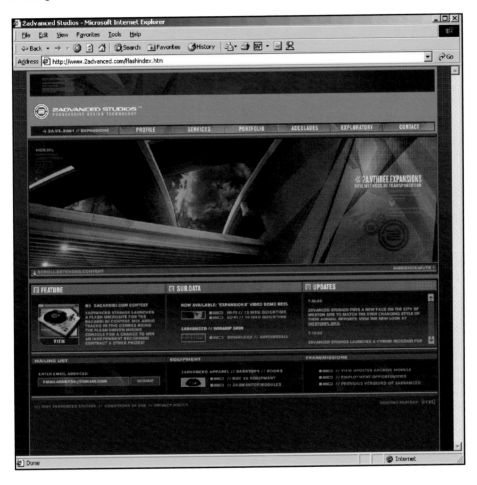

Extra Resources

The Help section within the Flash program provides a comprehensive set of tutorials as well as an ActionScript Dictionary and searchable help. The following sites should provide help with any other information you need when starting Flash development.

● Flash Kit provides a number of tutorials as well as an active forum, reviews, and resources for sound effects and sample movies. *http://www.flashkit.com*

- The Macromedia Designer & Developer Center has a section dedicated to Flash MX. It is regularly updated with examples and articles. *http://www.macromedia.com/desdev/mx/flash/*

- We're Here has a collection of tutorials and example movies as well as one of the most active Flash developers forums on the Web. *http://www.were-here.com/*

- Actionscript.org offers a comprehensive collection of tutorials and example movies for download. *http://www.actionscript.org/*

- Flazoom offers articles and editorials focused on Flash usability. *http://www.flazoom.com/news.shtml*

Now that we have looked at some of what is possible in Flash; in the next section we will explore Scalable Vector Graphics. At the end of the chapter we will look at some good practices to keep in mind when developing vector content for the Web as well as a comparison between the formats we have seen.

Scalable Vector Graphics (SVG)

Scalable Vector Graphics (SVG) was born in 1999 when the World Wide Web Consortium (WC3) started working on an open format for describing graphical objects in XML. The format has functionality for handling three types of graphic objects: vector shapes, text, and images.

SVG is a text-based format which means that, unlike a binary format like Flash, the graphics are read and written as text. Although a plugin is still needed to read SVG content, the implications of an XML-based text-based graphic format are exciting. For example, SVG has direct access to the browser's Document Object Model (DOM), which means it can interact with other page elements seamlessly. SVG objects can be controlled through HTML elements and vice versa. SVG's text-based nature also allows its content to be indexed by search engines, and it is also possible for anyone to view the underlying code of an SVG file just like viewing the source of an HTML document.

Being a W3C standard, the SVG format is designed to work closely with existing web technologies such as XML and Cascading Style Sheets (CSS), and the Document Object Model (DOM). SVG files are generally saved as an external file (with an .SVG file extension) and referenced through HTML although it is possible to integrate the SVG code directly into a HTML document. This technique - called "inline SVG" - is not well supported at the present, but over time it will become more widespread.

The SVG format allows for a full feature set of interactivity. Objects can be controlled through JavaScript or by using the SMIL (Synchronized Multimedia Integration Language) animation standard, which we will look at later in the chapter.

Although SVG is a long way behind Flash in terms of market penetration, it has significant support and contributions from industry. Until SVG viewers are included as standard on major browsers, plugins are needed to view SVG content - the most popular distribution being Adobe's SVG Player which now comes bundled with popular Adobe software such as Acrobat

A full list of SVG viewers is available at: *http://www.w3.org/Graphics/SVG/SVG-Implementations.htm8*

Creating SVG Graphics

At this stage there are two main ways to create SVG documents: using an SVG-capable graphics package, or marking up an SVG document in a text editor. In many cases it is a good idea to use both methods: create complex artwork in an illustration package then export to the SVG format where you can manipulate the markup and add interactivity.

SVG-Capable Graphics Packages

Because SVG graphics can be created in industry-standard graphics packages like Corel DRAW and Adobe Illustrator, it is possible to create SVG graphics without learning a line of code. Illustrator allows for native SVG reading and writing as well as maintaining the structure of the Illustrator document's symbols as `<symbol>` in the SVG markup. These illustration packages will allow for the creation of the graphics, but not for the adding of interactivity or animation

SVG-specific software like Jasc WebDraw allows for WYSIWYG editing, keyframe animations, and features a built-in SVG viewer. A trial version of WebDraw, as shown in the screenshot below, is available at: *http://www.jasc.com/products/webdraw/*

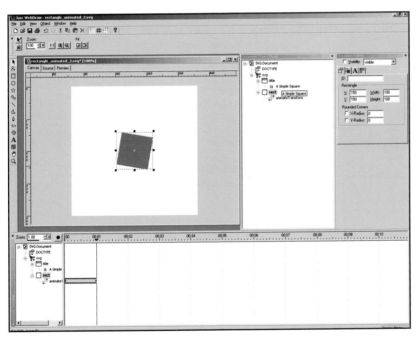

Products like WebDraw - currently at version 1 - will mature as the SVG format does, and other major packages will emerge to provide visual editing environments for SVG.

There are a broad range of utilities to create SVG content - such as Swift 3D which allows for export of 3D models from popular 3D software - but not a lot of visual editing environments that allow for animation and interactivity. A full list of SVG editors is available at the W3C SVG site.

Hand Coding

Although it is an advantage of the SVG format that no specific authoring software is needed to write the documents, creating SVG graphics by hand-coding is impractical for anything but simple shapes, so complex artwork should be exported from software like Corel DRAW or Adobe Illustrator.

Basic SVG Shape Elements

There are six basic shapes we can start playing with in SVG, and they are as follows:

- The `rect` element for rectangles
- The `circle` element for circles
- The `ellipse` element for ellipses
- The `line` element for lines
- The `polyline` element for open shapes
- The `polygon` element for closed shapes

The same shape we created in Flash earlier can be created with the 5 lines of SVG code that follow:

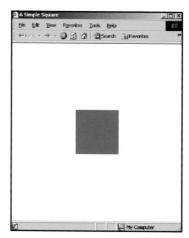

```
<?xml version="1.0" standalone="no"?>
<!DOCTYPE svg PUBLIC "-//W3C//DTD SVG 1.0//EN"
        "http://www.w3.org/TR/2001/REC-SVG-20010904/DTD/svg10.dtd">
<svg width="400" height="400">
<title>A Simple Square</title>
<rect x="150" y="150" width="100" height="100" style="fill:rgb(204,0,153)"
/>
</svg>
```

Those familiar with XML and/or CSS should recognize the properties in this example. The first two lines of an SVG document are always an XML declaration followed by the SVG doctype. The next line is the SVG root element. All SVG code must be contained within the `<svg>` tag much in the same way the HTML must be contained in the `<HTML>` tag. The width and height attributes of this tag define the dimensions of the canvas - or viewport - in which we will be working.

Inside the `<svg>` tag is the title and a definition of a square. The title tag works in exactly the same way that the title in HTML works. Using the `<rect>` shape element with attributes for x, y, width, height, and fill style creates the square. The x and y attributes mark the top-left corner of the image, within the canvas we declared in the `<svg>` tag.

In this example we have declared a fill style inline, but it is also possible to read a style from a CSS stylesheet to keep consistent styles throughout a whole document, or indeed multiple documents.

The following code achieves the same results by changing the inline style to a class and defining it at the top of the page in CSS. The CSS has to be defined within a CDATA section to separate non-XML portions of the document.

```
<?xml version="1.0" standalone="no"?>
<!DOCTYPE svg PUBLIC "-//W3C//DTD SVG 1.0//EN"
"http://www.w3.org/TR/2001/REC-SVG-20010904/DTD/svg10.dtd">
<svg width="400" height="400">
<style type="text/css"> <![CDATA[
.pink {fill:rgb(204,0,153)}
]]>
</style>
<title>A Simple Square</title>
<rect x="150" y="150" width="100" height="100" class="pink" />
</svg>
```

Creating a circle is as just as easy, although the `<circle>` element uses different attributes:

```
<?xml version="1.0" standalone="no"?>
<!DOCTYPE svg PUBLIC "-//W3C//DTD SVG 1.0//EN"
          "http://www.w3.org/TR/2001/REC-SVG-20010904/DTD/svg10.dtd">
<svg width="400" height="400">
<title>A Simple Circle</title>
<circle cx="150" cy="150" r="100" style="fill:rgb(204,0,153)" />
</svg>
```

The center of the circle is located using the cx and cy attributes, in the same way as the x and y attributes located the top-left corner of the square, and we define the radius of the circle with the r attribute. This produces the following result:

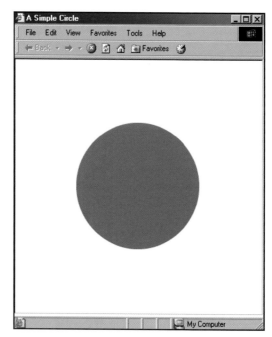

Comparing the file size to a simple BMP image of the same circle, the SVG file is 299 bytes, the bitmap is 99 Kilobytes - a significant difference. If we make the circle twice as large, the SVG file remains the same size; the bitmap file, however, becomes 241KB.

Because the examples we have used to demonstrate Flash and SVG are quite simple, the file sizes have turned out quite similar. The keyframe- and ActionScript- controlled Flash versions turned out to be 370 and 313 bytes respectively; the SVG version was 470 bytes.

Images

No graphic format would be complete without being able to import bitmap images. The SVG format uses the `<image>` element to import images in an almost identical way to HTML syntax.

```
<?xml version="1.0" standalone="no"?>
<!DOCTYPE svg PUBLIC "-//W3C//DTD SVG 1.0//EN"
"http://www.w3.org/TR/2001/REC-SVG-20010904/DTD/svg10.dtd">
<svg width="400" height="400">
<title>Donkey</title>
<desc>Image of a Donkey</desc>
<image x="100" y="100" width="140px" height="234px" xlink:href="donkey.png"
/>
</svg>
```

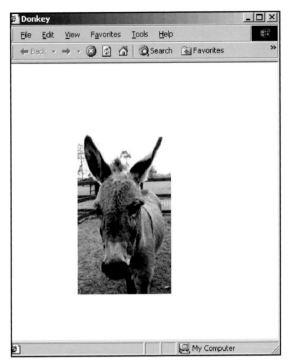

Scripting, Animation, and Interactivity

Like Flash, SVG has a fully featured set of properties, which can be animated or interacted with. SVG and Flash cross over in a number of different functions, but each has their own strengths. For example, SVG has the ability to add filters such as blurs, bevels, and textures to both vector and bitmap elements and animate them over time.

Because the SVG movies are part of the browser's DOM, SVG can communicate with other elements outside the SVG movie seamlessly.

Animation

Every element of an SVG document can be controlled with the SMIL animation standard or JavaScript with the DOM. Rather than being a timeline-based animation format like Flash, SVG uses timing (usually in seconds) for animations. Hand-coding complex interactive animations in a text editor will require a high level of programming experience, but making simple changes to an object's properties over time using the SMIL standard is surprisingly simple.

Let's look at replicating the animation we created in Flash earlier. The SMIL animation standard is quite like a code-based version of keyframe animation in that you define the properties to change how long it should take to do it, and points in between are generated automatically.

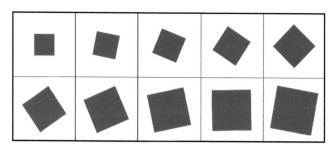

```
<?xml version="1.0"?>
<!DOCTYPE svg PUBLIC "-//W3C//DTD SVG 1.0//EN"
        "http://www.w3.org/TR/2001/REC-SVG-20010904/DTD/svg10.dtd">
<svg width="400" height="400">
        <rect x="150" y="150" width="100" height="100"
                style="fill:rgb(204,0,153)">
                <animate attributeName="x" attributeType="XML" begin="0s" dur="1s"
                        fill="freeze" from="150" to="100">
                </animate>
                <animate attributeName="y" attributeType="XML" begin="0s" dur="1s"
                        fill="freeze" from="150" to="100">
                </animate>
                <animate attributeName="width" attributeType="XML" begin="0s"
dur="1s" fill="freeze" from="100" to="200">
                </animate>
                <animate attributeName="height" attributeType="XML" begin="0s"
dur="1s" fill="freeze" from="100" to="200">
                </animate>
                <animateTransform attributeName="transform" begin="0s" dur="1s"
fill="freeze" calcMode="linear" type="rotate" additive="sum" from="0 200 200"
to="100 200 200"/>
        </rect>
</svg>
```

The first three lines remain unchanged, but we have added some animation elements inside the `<rect>` object. To keep it XML-compliant we have to remove the trailing slash from the `<rect>` tag, and add a closing tag `</rect>` at the end.

SVG has several different animation elements - `animate`, `set`, `animateMotion`, `animateColor` and `animateTransform`. In the example above, we have used animate to perform the positioning (x and y coordinates) and the scaling, while using the animateTransform for rotation.

While most animations can be changed using SVG's built-in animation properties, there are some circumstances where JavaScript and the Document Object Model must control it. This makes it possible to create non-linear animations (much like the site examples we looked at before in Flash) by making use of the `setInterval` function.

Example - Battlebots

The Battlebots site (*http:// www.battlebots.com*) has some excellent examples of interactive elements in SVG. This example shows animated elements from the robots and is made up of some 7,500 lines of code.

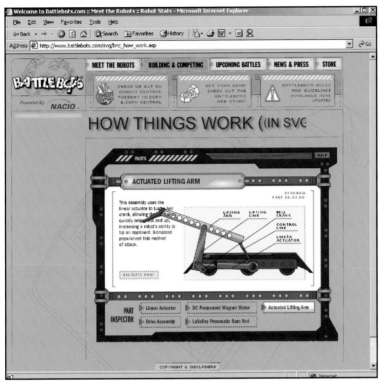

The file weighs in at 197Kb, and because SVG has no built-in functions for preloading or breaking up content it may take a while to load on some slower connections. Apart from the load times, it is an impressive example of the animation and interactive features of the SVG format.

Adding SVG to HTML Documents

Although it is possible to write SVG inline into HTML documents, this functionality is limited to a small number of browsers, platforms, and SVG players, so almost all SVG content is included into HTML pages using the `<embed>` tag. Below is an example of embedding the square we created in SVG into an HTML page:

```
<!DOCTYPE HTML PUBLIC "-//W3C//DTD HTML 4.0 Transitional//EN">
<html>
<head>
<title>A Simple Square</title>
</head>
<body>
<EMBED SRC="square.svg" NAME="A Simple Square" width="400" height="400"
TYPE="image/svg-xml" PLUGINSPAGE="http://www.adobe.com/svg/viewer/install/">
</body>
</html>
```

Extra Resources

Now that we have had a quick look at the drawing and animation functions in SVG you may want to explore some extra resources to learn more about the format.

- The **Adobe SVG Zone** has a good overview as well as tutorials and demos. *http://www.adobe.com/svg/*

- The **W3C SVG Homepage** has links to SVG-related news, software, and technical documents. *http://www.w3.org/Graphics/SVG/*

- A 30-day trial of the **Jasc Webdraw** SVG authoring tool is available for download from the Jasc web site. *http://www.jasc.com/products/webdraw/*

SMIL (Synchronized Multimedia Integration Language)

Like SVG, SMIL is a W3C standard markup language based on XML. The role of SMIL (Synchronized Multimedia Integration Language) is to synchronize the different media - video, audio, text, animation, and image - that make up multimedia presentations. The SMIL document does not seek to replace these media, nor does it actually contain any of them within the SMIL file, but rather act as a means to bring them all together.

Like SVG and HTML, SMIL is a text-based format, which means it is easy to create and edit - either as SMIL files or generated dynamically by server-side scripts. By generating SMIL dynamically it is possible to cater for complex customization.

The power of SMIL lies in integrating and synchronizing different media types. For example, it is possible to show a video and have captions or graphics appear over the top in the language of the viewer's choice, much in the same way as a DVD uses captions. At presentation time it is possible to show, hide, animate, or customize any element of a SMIL document.

SMIL also has built-in functions to customize playback based on the language, screen size, screen color depth, and bit-rate of the user's system using the *<switch>* tag.

If this doesn't sound exciting enough, there are already millions of users capable of viewing SMIL content. SMIL is supported through Real Player and QuickTime software, as well as numerous other SMIL-capable players. Internet Explorer 5.5 and 6 have support for HTML+TIME, which is based on the SMIL 2.0 working draft.

A full list of available players is listed at the W3C web site: *http://www.w3.org/AudioVideo/#SMIL*

Authoring SMIL

Although there are numerous applications that allow for creating and editing of SMIL documents within a visual environment, it is quite simple to create basic SMIL applications in a text editor.

There are currently six defined media types that can be included in SMIL movies:

- `<audio>`
- `<video>`
- `<image>`
- `<text>`
- `<textstream>`
- `<animation>`

Different SMIL players support different media formats within these types. For example, the Real Player can include RealVideo and RealAudio in SMIL, while the Quicktime player can include Quicktime audio and video. We'll discuss the interoperability between SMIL players a little later.

Let's have a look at creating a SMIL document that combines text and images in a two-part sequence.

```
<?xml version="1.0"?>
<smil xmlns="http://www.w3.org/2001/SMIL20/Language">
<head>
        <layout>
                <root-layout width="400" height="300" background-color="white"
/>
                <region id="donkeyimage" left="20" top="20" width="140"
height="234" background-color="white" />
                <region id="textarea" left="200" top="20" width="180"
height="280" background-color="white" fit="fill" />
        </layout>
</head>
<body>
        <text src="introduction.txt" region="textarea" dur="6s" />
        <par>
                <text src="png_description.txt" region="textarea" dur="6s" />
                <img src="donkey.png" alt="Donkey" region="donkeyimage"
dur="5s" begin="1s" />
        </par>
        </body>
</smil>
```

The first thing you'll notice is how similar the syntax is to HTML. Because it's an XML-based format like SVG, an XML declaration and the `<smil>` opening tag take up the first two lines. SMIL is also case-sensitive, meaning all tags must be written in lowercase.

The `<head>` section of the document contains elements for the layout areas of the documents or regions. These regions define the placement of all visual elements in the movie.

The root-layout tag defines the global layout properties of the document such as background color and size of the working area. The different region tags I have defined are assigned a unique name as well as size and position (measured in pixels from the top left of the screen, or in percentage). These regions are where we will add the different elements once we get to the body of the document.

Regions can use optional formatting attributes in the fit set such as fit-fill, meet, scroll, and slice to fit to the screen area as well as use the CSS-like z-index attribute to position elements over one another. For the textarea region we have used fit-fill which will allow the text to wrap.

The `<body>` section of the document represents the sequence of elements we are going to display on the screen. In this example I have imported text from the file **introduction.txt** and placed it inside the textarea region we defined in the head section of the document. The dur attribute describes how long we are going to show this element on screen before moving on to the next element in the sequence.

Elements included within a `<par>` tag like the next two elements in our document will display simultaneously - or in parallel. Once the player reaches the `<par>` tag, it allows everything within the tag to be displayed simultaneously, with optional attributes to have them start at different times.

We then have another area of text imported from the file **png_description.txt**, followed by the `<img>` element used to display the file donkey.png.

While video and audio elements have inbuilt time properties that define their duration, media elements such as text and image need the dur property set in order to define how long they are displayed on screen. You'll notice that the `<img>` element in this example contains attributes for both dur and begin. We have set begin to 1s which means that there is a delay of one second before the image appears.

Because QuickTime does not fully support the whole SMIL specification, there are some inconsistencies in the way it formats the regions. Here is how the file looks in RealOne player:

The appearance of the first part of the presentation, which uses the `<text>` tag.

The second part of the SMIL document uses `<img>` and `<text>` tags in parallel.

SMIL Players

While the SMIL format is a standard defined by the W3C, the media players which can play back SMIL content support different types of media. RealNetworks' RealOne has comprehensive support for the basic file formats like text, GIF, and JPEG, but also supports the use of its proprietary formats - RealAudio, RealVideo, RealText etc. - within SMIL content. Likewise Apple's QuickTime Player cannot play RealAudio and RealVideo, but can play QuickTime video and audio files.

Neither RealOne nor QuickTime support the SVG format natively, but RealOne can download an SVG plugin to view SVG content. Flash content can be played in RealOne or QuickTime using the `<animation>` tag.

When authoring specifically for QuickTime Player, you can save a SMIL file with the .MOV extension. In order to have QuickTime understand the SMIL file, we just add the 8-character string SMILtext to the first line of the document above the XML declaration.

Because SMIL is an extensible format, it allows for player-specific code to be added to the SMIL documents. For example QuickTime players can add or remove the slider using `qt:time-slider="true"` or enable autoplay using `qt:autoplay="true"` within the `<smil>` tag.

Reference

We have only explored a small part of SMIL's capabilities, and there is a great deal more to the format. The following resources are a good place to start learning more.

- The W3C SMIL Page offers a link to SMIL documentation as well as the full specifications. *http://www.w3.org/AudioVideo/*

- W3C Draft SMIL specification. *http://www.w3.org/TR/smil20/*

- Real Networks Production Guide includes a comprehensive look at authoring SMIL as well as a tag guide. *http://service.real.com/help/library/guides/realone/ProductionGuide/realpgd.htm*

- The Inside QuickTime: Interactive Movies PDF file on the Apple developer site provides insight into developing interactive movies within the QuickTime format.
  http://developer.apple.com/techpubs/quicktime/qtdevdocs/PDF/insideqt_intmov.pdf

Now that we have explored the different formats, let's take a look at some key differences between the main vector formats - Flash and SVG.

Key Differences between Flash and SVG

Now that we have had a look at what Flash and SVG are capable of, let's have a look at the key differences between the formats. Although both are capable of producing similar results, there are a number of fundamental differences between the two that should be taken into account when choosing a format to author with.

Binary versus Text-Based

When you author a SWF file from Flash, you are actually compiling a binary file that cannot be de-compiled and/or edited again. SVG files are text-based from the time they are written to the time they are rendered. The source of an SVG file can be viewed just like an HTML file, or edited on a server to generate server-side dynamic graphics.

The fact that SVG is text-based also holds significant advantages for interactivity. For example, JavaScript functions could be written to write whole SVG movies into the browser window on demand. Likewise certain browsers and SVG viewers will allow for XHTML to be written inside SVG documents. The support for "inline" SVG (code written directly into an XHTML page) is still low, but that will change as acceptance for the format grows.

Authoring Software

Although support for creating static SVG files in illustration applications such as Corel DRAW and Adobe Illustrator is improving, at this stage there is no SVG animation tool to match the features and ease of use of Macromedia's Flash.

One of the best visual editors for SVG creation is WebDraw by Jasc that we looked at briefly earlier. Webdraw contains a timeline, sourcecode view and preview window that opens your SVG file in an Internet Explorer shell inside the application.

A full list of SVG authoring software is available at: *http://www.w3.org/Graphics/SVG/SVG-Implementations.htm8*

Player Software

Even though the Flash Player format is open, the majority of people viewing Flash are using the official Macromedia Flash Player, which is available for all major platforms including mobile devices. The file size of the Adobe SVG player is quite large in comparison to the Flash player (2.3Mb vs. 400kb) and at the current time there is just not enough awareness or compelling content for users to justify downloading it.

Macromedia claim that their Flash player is installed on over 90% of all Internet users' computers, compared with around 10% for SVG players.

A full list of software and operating systems on which the Flash Player is installed as standard is available at: *http://www.macromedia.com/software/player_census/flashplayer/partners.html*

Filters, Paths, and Objects

The SVG format includes filters for both vector and bitmap objects that can be animated over time, so you could add a blur or similar effect if you want. Flash does not include any filters, so the only way to achieve such effects is to create separate images and import each one into the timeline.

While artwork for both Flash and SVG can be created in standard vector drawing packages such as Illustrator, FreeHand, or Corel DRAW, the way they treat paths and shapes is quite different. Because SVG can access all of the elements that make up the file, SVG developers have more control of individual elements such as bezier curves.

Integration with Standard Technologies

Because Flash is a binary format that is merely embedded into an HTML page, its properties cannot easily be controlled from outside the Flash movie on the client. SVG's properties are all available to be manipulated through the browser's DOM.

Audio and Video Support

The SVG format has no built-in support for sound or video, though by combining SVG with SMIL it is possible to use linked audio or video files. Flash, on the other hand, has extensive support for streaming video and high-quality audio files, as well as capturing video and audio from a client's webcams.

Issues When Dealing with Vector Graphics on the Web

As with all things on the Web, using vector graphics is not without pitfalls. Let's explore some of the main issues you should consider when authoring vector graphics.

Vector Graphics Are Not for Everything

Although we have seen some of the benefits of developing in vector formats in this chapter, authoring in HTML is often a better solution. Neither SVG or Flash are particularly good at presenting large amounts of text-based information, and the user often cannot scroll within the movies using the scrollbar on their mouse. Both SVG and Flash formats are more difficult to develop for and less standard than HTML for the simple delivery of information.

There is also the issue of accessibility. Unless properly authored, vector formats can be inaccessible to those viewing the Web through screen readers and other assistive technologies. Macromedia added an Accessibility palette to Flash MX, which makes it possible to assign text equivalents to graphical objects. They have also set up an Accessibility Resource Center where developers can learn how to make their Macromedia-authored content more accessible.
http://www.macromedia.com/macromedia/accessibility/

An additional disadvantage of Flash is that it isn't indexed as well by search engines as plain text; an important point to remember if you're considering creating a whole site in Flash. Similarly, if search engines cannot view key areas of content or navigation, you could be missing out on those all-important rankings, an important consideration if using Flash for animated navigation or any form of content.

Check for the Necessary Plugins

The fact is that at this point in time, not everybody is going to have the plugins or viewers necessary to view vector image content, so it is essential to detect the presence of a plugin on the user's browser. This may change over time if SVG or Flash viewers are installed as standard in all browsers, but it is going to be a long timebefore that happens, if it happens at all.

To prevent users without the necessary plugin from trying to view vector content (and to provide them with an alternative) you can either inform the user that they will need a plugin to view the content you are going to show, or detect if they have that plugin installed. Using a detection script like the ones listed below allows the user to be alerted if they need additional or upgraded software to view the content on your page, but importantly, it will take those who do have the plugin straight to the content they came for.

- **Macromedia's Flash Deployment Kit:**
  http://www.macromedia.com/software/flash/download/deployment_kit/

- **Colin Moock's Flash player Inspector:**
  http://www.moock.org/webdesign/flash/detection/moockfpi/

- **Sun's SVG detection script:** *http://wwws.sun.com/software/xml/developers/svg/support/*

If the user does not have the plugin they need, it is important you display at least some alternative content. There are certainly some examples where it is not possible to deliver in alternative formats, but if you provide some content and a link to where the user can download the plugin, the may user return to the site when they have the appropriate software.

With formats continually upgrading their players, it is often best to author for the second most recent release in order to reach a wider audience. Flash 5 has somewhere in the order of two to three times more installed viewers than Flash player 6.

Be Conscious of File Size

Some developers spend too much time using the power of interactive file formats and not enough time testing on the Internet connection their users will be viewing them on. This is certainly not the fault of the format, but developers should be aware of their audience and how long it takes to download a file from the average user's modem.

Bitmap images embedded or referenced from Flash or SVG movies still need to be compressed appropriately as do music and video tracks in Flash. Complex vector shapes should be simplified in either illustration software or within the authoring environment.

Flash has good functionality to deal with loading rich content including preload scripts and streaming separate SWF movies into a "shell", so it is worthwhile planning how to break content up before starting production on a Flash project.

If you are using Flash, don't embed more typefaces than you need. Apart from this being good design practice, a typeface adds between 10 to 20Kb to the size of a movie when you embed fonts.

Avoid Unnecessary Animations

Remember the goals of the site you are developing and work out whether the animation is benefiting the user. Some users will be impressed with animations of corporate logos set to music tracks, but most of the time they just want to get to the content and will become irritated with unnecessary animations - particularly if they are return visitors.

If you want to get to an important document, it can be frustrating waiting for an animated menu to unfold before you can even get to it. If you do choose to create splash screens or animations that disrupt people from getting to the information, it is a good idea to provide a "*skip*" button.

Vectors Can Be CPU-Intensive

A computer's CPU has to render the vector graphics to the screen as pixels, if there are too many shapes and paths, this can place a heavy load on the computer. The problem is amplified when dealing with animated vector graphics. While your animations may look spectacular on computers with modern CPUs and graphics cards, older hardware may have trouble rendering the animations at the speeds they were intended.

Processing long strings or XML data on the client-side can also be quite CPU-intensive, so it is worthwhile testing performance on different platforms. Colin Moock's "FPS Speedometer" tests the frame rate of a user's computer, so you can deliver alternative content for users with older hardware; it can be found at: *http://www.moock.org/webdesign/flash/actionscript/fps-speedometer/index.html*

Summary

As we've seen, vector graphics are fundamentally different from bitmap images, and each has its advantages and disadvantages. The formats we have looked at in this chapter can combine vector graphics with bitmap images to create animations, presentations, or whole sites.

Vector graphics formats can offer significant advantages over bitmap graphics and HTML layout in certain situations, but are not without their flaws. We have discussed how best to use the formats and the issues to consider when developing in Flash and SVG.

This is only an introduction to the formats discussed, and we have suggested some resources that you can explore to expand your knowledge.

Index

A Guide to the Index

The index is arranged alphabetically in word-by-word order (so that New York would sort before Newark), with symbol prefixes ignored. Acronyms have been preferred to their expansions as main entries because they are easier to recall. Unmodified headings generally indicate the fullest treatment of a topic; sub-entries lead to specific aspects. Comments specifically on the index will be welcome at billj@glasshaus.com.

D

E

example web pages (Con'd)

F

N

O

S

V

v2288.reactive.com, 117
vector graphics, 201
    bitmap graphics compared to, 202
    creating using Fireworks, 185
    Flash and SVG as vector formats, 166
    formats, 203-233
        Macromedia Flash, 204
        SVG (Scalable Vector Graphics), 220
    issues to consider, 233
    principles, 202
vector-based design styles, 117
verse, 64
victoriassecret.com site, 26
visible and off-screen layout elements, 126
visual elements
    action components, 104
    applying color, 51
    associating grouped elements, 131
    content components, 94
    layout components, 85
visual grids as alignment aids, 155
visual impairment
    see also accessibility.
    accessibility of text as images, 66
    indicating required form fields, 103
    resources, 46
    suitable color combinations, 45
    text-based information and, 114
VML (Vector Markup Language), 202

W

W3C (World Wide Web Consortium)
    see also SVG; SMIL.
    CSS specification, 73
    HTML 4.01 element listing, 68
    SMIL Page, 231
    SVG Homepage, 228
W3Schools.com site, browser use statistics, 134
WAP (Wireless Application Protocol) devices, 16

watermark response to weak branding, 95
web graphics
    see also graphic design.
    basic technology and terminoology, 6
    charactersitics of effective graphics, 10
    key concepts, 5
web pages
    see also example web pages.
    device-specific alternative pages, 16
    general rules for typography, 60
webdesign-l.com site, 197
WebDraw, JASC Software, 221, 228, 232
webmonkey article on web-safe colors, 40
webpagesthatsuck.com site, 15
web-safe palettes, 38
    color shifts with 15-bit hardware, 40
    death of the web-safe color palette, 40
    Photoshop GIF optimization, 183
    recommended for backgrounds, 40
weight, typefaces, 60
Weinman, Lynda, web-safe palette publicist, 38
welcome messages, 104
were-here.com site, 220
white space around graphics, 13
    see also padding; spacing.
    mouse targeting and, 14
width attribute, <img> element, 7, 174
wishlist.com.au site, 34, 50, 106, 138
WLRLaw.com site, 103
wrapping text around graphics with align, 8

X

xbox.com site, 151
x-heights, 57
XHTML, 68
    SVG and, 232
XML (Extensible Markup Language)
    SMIL based on, 228
    SVG based on, 220

Z

ZC Sterling web site, 15